The Many Ways of Light

Lam Partners

The Many Ways of Light

Preface by Moshe Safdie

Preface | *Moshe Safdie*   7
Introduction   11

Selected Projects

   Kauffman Center for the Performing Arts   16
   Crystal Bridges Museum of American Art   24
   David L. Lawrence Convention Center   30
   Phipps Conservatory and Botanical Gardens   36
   United States Institute of Peace   42
   Boston Public Library Johnson Building   48
   Main Street Station   56
   International Law Office   62
   Qaumajuq–Inuit Art Centre, Winnipeg Art Gallery   68
   Liberty Mutual Tower   76
   Dickies Arena   84
   Boston City Hall Renovation   92
   Public Realm   98
   Paul L. Foster Campus for Business and Innovation, Baylor University   106
   The National Memorial for Peace and Justice   112
   Cleveland Clinic Cancer Institute   118
   Yad Vashem: The World Holocaust Remembrance Center   124
   MIT Media Lab, Massachusetts Institute of Technology   130
   Salt Lake City Public Library   136
   Guggenheim Bilbao Museum   142
   Harry Reid International Airport   148
   Austin United States Courthouse   154
   Free Library of Philadelphia   158
   The Tower at PNC Plaza   164
   New World Center   170
   SoFi Stadium   176

Acknowledgments   187
Project credits   188
Current and past team members   191

Preface

Moshe Safdie

There are many ways of light. Natural light, originating from the sun, penetrating the buildings through windows and skylights, screens, and apertures; diffused and reflected. With direct sunlight come the many ways of shadows. The lace-like shadow patterns of trellises; the rhythmic patterns of colonnades; reflected ripples off a pond upon a wall. Then there is light generated by candles, by flames.

Electrically powered fixtures vary greatly, shining directly on surfaces, reflecting off surfaces, and lamps generating a wide range of colors of the spectrums. While historically we have aimed as much as possible to depend on daylight, from time immemorial, we have been dependent on generating light at night.

We tend to think of a lighting designer as primarily engaged in designing artificial lighting systems, focused on the diversity of potential sources, placement of the fixtures, calculating and measuring lighting levels. But the reality is that contemporary buildings, across almost all typologies, are lit by a combination of daylight and artificial light. Even on the brightest days we are dependent on artificial light, and more so as daylight fades away.

This deep understanding that designing lighting is about negotiating a delicate balance between daylight and artificial light is what drew Safdie Architects to Lam Partners almost 40 years ago. We first collaborated on Morgan Hall at the Harvard Business School, working then with the firm's founder and namesake, William Lam. Lam had studied the optimal light for the workspace. As office buildings became deeper, and workspaces further from daylight, Lam appreciated the need to provide ample light for the tasks on hand, with special emphasis on the appropriate source, realizing that direct fixtures create reflections and glare for people working on screens. Lam was cognizant of the stress created by glare, thus pioneering the illumination of workspaces by reflecting light off surfaces, particularly ceilings.

At Morgan Hall—designed to accommodate the faculty, doctoral candidates, and executive assistants of Harvard Business School—we embraced the motto that each and every person working in the building would have the pleasure and joy of some daylight. But Lam also recognized the need for effective supplemental artificial light. We worked together toward achieving a seamless interplay between the two. The building's central atrium became the source of light for many of the support staff, with Lam-designed computerized tracking mirrors below the skylights to direct sunlight to the depth of the courtyards.

This first collaboration led to a closer partnership spanning decades, working on some 20 major projects—academic buildings, hospitality, performing arts centers,

Albert Einstein Education and Research Center, São Paulo, Brazil

museums, residences, memorials. Each typology introduced its own particular and specific set of issues and challenges. I will demonstrate specifically through some of these case studies the extraordinary sensitivity and innovative spirit that the Lam Partners team has evolved and implemented over the years.

No building type is as demanding and challenging to a lighting designer than a museum. Given the building's purpose to display art and artifacts, the question of the source and quality of light is paramount. Museums stand and fall on how both their exhibits and their public spaces are lit. Museums also bring to the forefront the controversy over the appropriateness of natural versus artificial light as a source for illuminating the art. Moreover, it is further complicated by the varying requirements to conservation: the appropriate lighting source and levels for paintings on canvas, for works on paper, sculptures, and textiles. The optimal color of light and its intensity are fundamental to a successful patron experience. There are curators and indeed architects who believe that the expeditious approach is to create black-box galleries totally lit by artificial light as the best controllable way. Lam Partners and our team are believers and advocates of the sublime experience that can be achieved when art is lit naturally.

Museum lighting solutions require a careful balance between natural and artificial light, and the gentle transition from day and night. Studying the subtleties of the color of light between skylights that face north or south, or mixed light—direct and reflected light versus diffused light, we explored together ways to bring light free of shadows and streaking. Balancing the appropriate coloration of artificial light and natural light as it changes through the hours of the day.

Over the years we have collaborated with Lam Partners on several museums beginning with the Skirball Cultural Center in Los Angeles, followed by, in sequence, Khalsa Heritage Memorial Complex (now known as Virasat-e-Khalsa) in India, Telfair Museums' Jepson Center in Savannah, Yad Vashem: The World Holocaust Remembrance Center in Israel, and finally Crystal Bridges Museum of American Art, built in two phases, in Bentonville, Arkansas. Each of these museums introduced new and specific lighting requirements as each project was specific to place and program.

Crystal Bridges, which opened in 2011 and is now being dramatically expanded given its great success, presented the lighting designer with a wide range of opportunities. With much of the gallery ceiling being constructed entirely of Arkansas pine, the lighting seized on the warmth of the wood to create an ambiance unlike most museums. The galleries and public spaces are lit by reflecting light upon these wood surfaces with the overall effect of gentle warmth and intimacy throughout the museum. Set in the lush Ozark landscape with trails

From left to right: Kauffman Center for the Performing Arts; Crystal Bridges Museum of American Art

and ponds, the exterior lighting was delicately deployed to enhance the indoor-outdoor connections that have become the hallmark of the museum, and it opens, as evenings descend, dramatic views of the landscapes within the building as well as powerful displays of the life within.

Another typology in which Lam Partners has gone back to first principles is the garden atria, which has become the centerpiece of many of our institutional buildings. The challenge is to establish lighting levels that will allow plant life to thrive, while ensuring a comfortable level of temperature and humidity for people. At the Albert Einstein Education and Research Center in São Paulo, we explored the use of variable fritting on the skylight glazing, ranging from dense to open patterns depending on whether the areas below were planted or used heavily by the students and faculty. The resulting effect evokes the feeling of congregating under a leafy tree. The supplemental artificial lighting system for daytime and nighttime elegantly mixes the two and creates a gentle transformation, and the character of the garden atria, and the building as a whole, changes dramatically.

In two seminal projects, Yad Vashem and the Children's Memorial located on Mount Herzl in Jerusalem, lighting becomes an instrument that evokes emotions as the story unfolds. The Children's Memorial deployed "the many ways of light" but also of darkness. Upon entering the memorial, one is greeted by a series of floating black-and-white photographs of children who perished in the Holocaust. Proceeding down the path into the underground chamber, darkness descends. As the eye adjusts, we see millions of floating lights. A single candle in the center of the space, surrounded by semi-reflective glass and mirrored walls, floors, and ceilings, amplifies the candle into an infinity of floating lights. One moves through the chamber as the names of the murdered children are recited, exiting on the side of the opposite hill to light and life.

The historic museum consists of a series of underground galleries that straddle a prismatic-shaped linear path cutting into the mountain from the east and emerging on the west. A few skylights sparsely penetrate the mountain to light the galleries below, diffusing a soft glow over the artificially lit exhibits rich with films, photographs, and objects sensitive to light. More about the presence of the light than its actual role in lighting the exhibits, it is a reminder that you are in the depths of the earth. Only within the linear prism is there a continuous skylight leading toward the eruption of the structure overlooking Jerusalem Forest, shifting to a more joyous and celebratory topology.

At Kauffman Center for the Performing Arts in Kansas City, Lam Partners demonstrated its capacity to work dramatically different scales in concert with one another. Within the center are a dedicated concert hall and performance theater, each with its own set of lighting requirements. For the Muriel Kauffman Theatre, we worked with Lam to light the cast resin panels on the fascia of the three tiers of box seats to produce a stunning shimmering effect.

At the building scale, the sculptural masses of the hall and theater are dramatically lit on the exterior, enhancing the character of the building as night descends. From the north, the lighting of the arch structures makes them appear as a musically inspired geometry. From the south, the dramatically lit lobby acts as a chandelier overlooking the city.

What exemplifies the philosophy and methodology of Lam Partners is approaching each project, building type, and the specificity of site with a fresh and inquisitive eye while drawing on immense experience and knowledge. Lam always returns to first principles to explore the specific problem and conceive solutions that have resounding impact. In each case consideration is given to mood, the programmed activities, the functional requirements, basic issues of safety and performance, as well as the efficiency of energy consumption and maintainability of systems over time. Above all Lam Partners brings to buildings the sensibility and aesthetic that enhance our experience, uplifting the spirit.

Introduction

Light breathes life into architecture. In illuminating surfaces and spaces, light allows us to experience the practical and poetic qualities of architecture—its forms, materials, textures, and nuances—as we go about our daily routines of work, school, play, and other activities. Light is a key ingredient in shaping our perception of a building or exterior environment. Great lighting can guide us through a sequence of spaces, create the appropriate atmosphere for a given setting, influence our mood, add visual comfort and even delight. For more than 60 years, Lam Partners has evolved the art and science of architectural lighting to transform buildings and spaces, creating a lively and meaningful conversation between people, their surroundings, and light.

Lam Partners: The Many Ways of Light features 25 of our more recent and significant projects, as well as a selection of legacy and public realm projects completed over the years. Every building or exterior environment has a story to tell, and each of these experiences has provided us with rich memories and valuable lessons that have remained long after the project is complete.

It's been a challenging process to distil our legacy down to 25 signature examples of our work. The projects showcased best represent Lam Partners as a firm and exemplify our integrated design approach. It is not the lighting that stands out, but the beautiful architecture that we help celebrate. The projects comprise a variety of cultural, civic, commercial, educational, medical, and infrastructure works, including the Guggenheim Bilbao Museum, Yad Vashem, Salt Lake City Public Library, SoFi Stadium, and the United States Institute of Peace, all consistent with our integrated design approach. With daylight and electric light woven into the buildings, they illustrate how lighting and architecture work together to shape space and function and influence moods and emotions.

Lam Partners has had the great fortune to work with renowned architects Moshe Safdie, Frank Gehry, Fumihiko Maki, and Rafael Viñoly, among many others. We take pride in being an integral part of the architectural teams that create meaningful and memorable buildings and spaces for users to enjoy.

A selection of significant legacy projects is also included: Washington Metropolitan Area Transit Authority Stations, Custom House Tower, Massachusetts State House, and Washington Union Station. Designed by William (Bill) Lam, our founding president, these legacy projects are considered some of his greatest contributions to our profession and they set the foundation for what Lam Partners continues to do today. Modern technology has changed, but our values and principles have not. It has always been, and will always be, about designing for people.

Our History

The origins of Lam Partners began in 1949 when William M. C. Lam, better known as Bill Lam, founded Lam Workshop. After graduating from the Massachusetts Institute of Technology with a degree in architecture, Bill started exploring ideas to produce quality and economical architectural light fixtures and furniture, with forms driven by function and a clear understanding of the manufacturing process. In 1951, he changed the name of Lam Workshop to Lam Lighting Systems Inc., and produced a line of commercial-grade light fixtures that supported contemporary architectural expression and needs.

A decade later, Bill returned to his passion for architectural design. He founded William Lam Associates in 1961 and blazed the trail in the field of modern lighting design. Bill worked with architects around the United States and throughout the world, developing innovative lighting solutions and integrated systems for architecture and urban design. He believed in "lighting by design, not engineering," and celebrated the architecture through indirect lighting that concealed the presence of lighting hardware. This philosophy flowed from Bill's focus on the importance of quality illumination and his desire to capture the spirit and intent of the architect's vision.

Bill also believed in teamwork among architects, engineers, interior designers, and all the critical members involved in the design process. He would bring all disciplines together at the start of a project to orchestrate the creation of more beautiful spaces with truly integrated building systems and design approaches, as opposed to simply layering each on top of another. Bill was also very mindful that indirect lighting and quality over quantity were hugely important for sustainability and saving energy.

Robert Osten and Paul Zaferiou became partners with Bill in 1990, and the name of the firm changed to Lam Partners to recognize this transition. Keith Yancey became a principal in 2005, Glenn Heinmiller in 2008. They have since been joined by Justin Brown, James Perry, Matt Latchford, and Sarah Fisher in recent years.

After Bill retired in 1995, he maintained a small consulting business to pursue projects of special interest until his death in 2012. *Architectural Lighting* inducted Bill into its 2001 Hall of Fame, and his books *Perception and Lighting as Formgivers for Architecture* (1977) and *Sunlighting as Formgiver for Architecture* (1986), which outlined Bill's architectural lighting principles, continue to shape Lam Partners' work and the lighting design industry as we know it today.

Clockwise from top left: Custom House Tower; Massachusetts State House; Washington Union Station; Washington Metropolitan Area Transit Authority Stations

Lam Labs was founded as a division of Lam Partners in 2014, under the direction of Senior Associate Dan Weissman. Continuing Lam's tradition of challenging the boundaries of lighting, Lam Labs researches and explores innovative lighting ideas to create and communicate light in novel and meaningful ways.

In 2018, Lam Partners joined with studioi of Pittsburgh, established by Steve Iski in 2003. The two firms share design philosophies and a similarity of client types and project portfolios, and the strength of the firm has grown through this collaborative partnership.

Lam Partners Today

Lam Partners marked its 60th anniversary in 2021. Our talented and passionate group of designers is based in Cambridge, Pittsburgh, and now in several satellite locations around the United States. We have evolved a collaborative culture that defines our practice and values, with an interdisciplinary team trained as architects, architectural engineers, interior designers, and industrial designers. We pride ourselves in clear conceptual thinking, creative problem solving, and pooling our wealth of knowledge and experience to make every project a success. Without hierarchy or ego involved, the best ideas put forward by any team member shape our design solutions.

Building on Lam Partners' history of integrated lighting, we become an essential part of the architectural team. Design sessions are charged with creative energy, storytelling, and yes—even sketching! Ideas are explored and tested, details drawn, fixtures evaluated, and strategies devised to produce meaningful and expressive lighting designs. Cutting-edge techniques and computer visualization capabilities—many developed in-house—as well as real-world mock-ups, are used to test and refine installations. Solutions are explored and crafted to bring daylighting and electric lighting—the two essential parts of any building—together as a unified whole. Through our work, we find that a well-organized lighting system often informs the architectural design, helping to resolve inconsistencies, leading to interesting patterns, effects, and a serendipitous beauty that may not have initially been conceived.

Lam Partners works across a broad range of project types, implementing a variety of technical and creative daylighting and electric lighting strategies. We use methods to analyze and shape the daylighting in interior spaces for useful illumination, and integrate electric lighting without visible hardware, so that the architecture, not the light source, is seen as the source of illumination. Ever mindful of energy efficiency and sustainability, lighting strategies are designed

From left to right: David L. Lawrence Convention Center; Cleveland Clinic Cancer Institute; SoFi Stadium

and fixtures are selected to reduce and minimize energy consumption. While a great deal of effort is focused on the design process, much time is also spent managing the construction phase of each project, including jobsite meetings and visits to ensure that the lighting concepts and details are executed as intended.

Lighting hardware and design tools have certainly changed through the decades and generations. Our industry has evolved through several lighting revolutions, from incandescent to fluorescent to metal halide and now to LED technology. Computer capabilities have advanced tremendously, but the principles and foundations of good lighting design remain the same as we prioritize the human experience and quality illumination. Lam's approach to architectural lighting still begins with understanding the vision of the architect and owner.

Lam Partners is committed to building rewarding, collaborative, and lasting relationships with the existing and emerging design community. As educators, we believe in the exchange of information, sharing our knowledge with architects and clients, and presenting solutions and opportunities. Through our teaching in local architecture schools and mentoring new members of the Lam team, we seek to actively nurture the next generation of talent in our profession. Moving forward, our vision is to continue to demonstrate leadership in the profession with our integrated approach to architectural lighting design. Every project is an opportunity to make the built environment better with light.

Kauffman Center for the Performing Arts

Kansas City, Missouri

With its soaring glass-enclosed lobby and sculpted, segmented shells, Kauffman Center for the Performing Arts is a striking addition to downtown Kansas City. A very precise and targeted lighting approach reveals and articulates the forms and details of the building designed by Safdie Architects and celebrates the experience and excitement of attending a performance or event.

Moshe Safdie designed two entry sequences into the expansive glass lobby. Visitors can arrive from the north through a canyon-like slot between the two sculpted shell forms, or via the formal entry to the south, where low-level bollards light the drop-off and narrow spotlights shimmer up the tension cables like the strings of a harp.

The daylit glass lobby is bright and airy and mimics the changes of natural light throughout the day. At night, it becomes a more dramatic setting, illuminated by the architectural elements defining the volume. Narrow spotlights wash down the tall, angled columns along the glass curtain wall. On the opposite side, illuminated balcony walls reflect the curvature of the performance halls. Downlights on the balconies bounce light off the blue and red carpeting, tinting the ceilings with a playful indirect glow.

There is festive exuberance in the Muriel Kauffman Theatre where the balcony fronts sparkle and shimmer. Evoking the chandeliers of grand, traditional theaters, this concept emerged from the vision of a central chandelier bursting outwards to become the face of the balconies. The glimmering effect is created with textured acrylic forms backed by folded reflective metal and internal illumination. Colorful geometric murals, designed and painted by Kansas City Art Institute students, are illuminated behind wood slat walls around the theater that serve as part of the acoustical tuning system.

Helzberg Hall has a more intimate, immersive atmosphere, with a soft ambient glow across the curving wood walls and dynamic light animating the back of the stage. Daylight filters through skylights and down the curved flutes, interacting with ribbons of metal mesh to spectacular effect. This effect is extended into the night as electric fixtures in the skylights send streaks down the back of the stage.

Outside, floodlights in the landscape illuminate the building at night, articulating the segmented forms of the sculpted shells. By lighting the architectural forms, inside and outside, Kauffman Center for the Performing Arts becomes a distinctive civic landmark in downtown Kansas City, and elevates the experience of music, theater, and performance.

Lobby columns are defined by spotlights mounted to the tubular beam, and carefully aimed floodlights provide general illumination and even coverage. The color wash on the balcony walls is created by light reflected from the carpet—a planned effect achieved through elaborate testing.

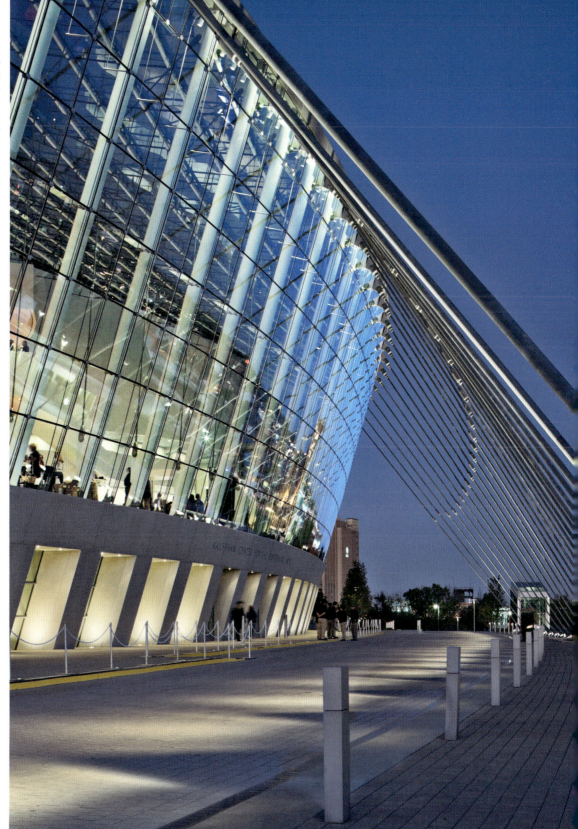

Very narrow accent lights illuminate the cornice and cables rising above the formal drop-off. Forward-throw bollards light the driveway surface, and LED marker lights identify the curb, aligning with each column above.

Clusters of carefully aimed floodlights placed among the prairie grass provide a soft, even wash across the sides of the building, and articulate the segmented forms of the sculpted shells.

The ceiling in Helzberg Hall floats, detached from the walls by a curving light slot filled with closely spaced monopoint wallwashers. The complex curving forms of the ceilings in both the concert hall and theater were a challenge for locating fixtures. All the recessed fixtures are accessible from a catwalk located above.

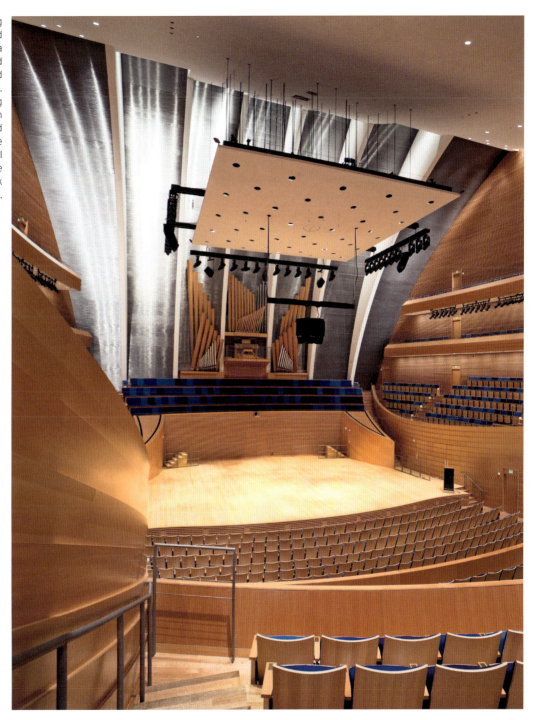

"Exploded chandeliers" adorn the balcony fronts, with dimmable LED strips varying the intensity of light and sparkle effect. Trimless pinholes under balconies and downlights in high ceilings can be tuned throughout, and monopoint wallwashers eliminate any sense of darkness at the back of the balconies.

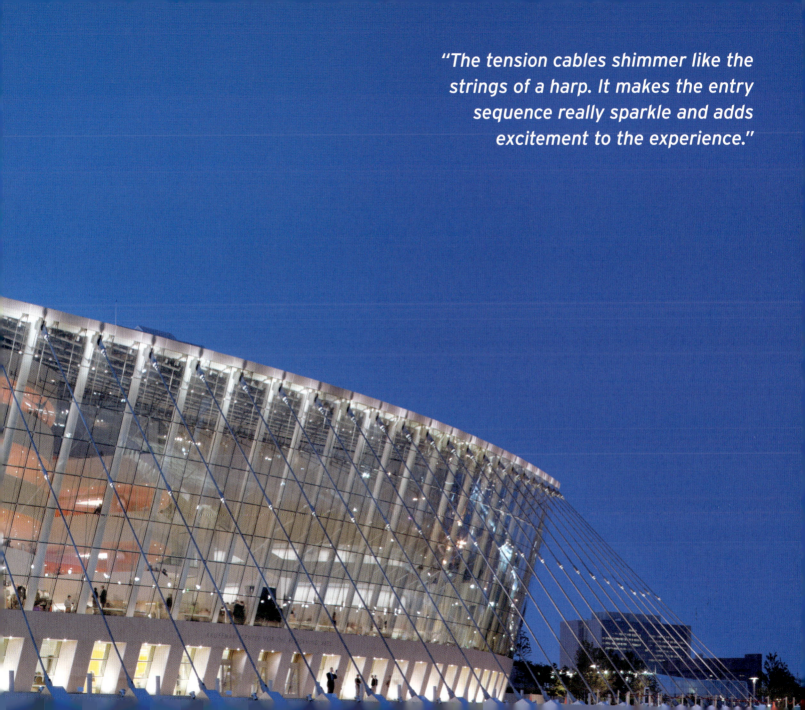

"The tension cables shimmer like the strings of a harp. It makes the entry sequence really sparkle and adds excitement to the experience."

Crystal Bridges Museum of American Art

Bentonville, Arkansas

Nestled within a river valley in the foothills of the Ozark Mountains, Crystal Bridges Museum of American Art is a departure from the typical museum-going experience. Designed by Safdie Architects, the museum is a series of pavilions that respond to the essence of the place and the site, offering an immersive environment that intertwines the beauty of nature and art. Lam worked with Safdie to develop the integrated lighting systems that work in harmony with the spirit and form of the gently curving architecture, natural environment, and the unique gallery experience.

The pavilions circulate around and over a stream, with the two pavilion bridges creating a holding pond with weirs below. As visitors move through the pavilions and cross the pond, they pass through glass-enclosed links between the galleries, where art and nature can be experienced harmoniously.

Echoing the rolling Ozarks, the pavilions have rounded roofs and curving wood ceilings that sweep upward or form a vaulted shape. The integrated lighting system between the exposed Glu-lam beams mimics the curving geometries of each roof to reinforce the architectural forms. The simple, cohesive scheme pairs accent lighting and indirect lighting in curved metal assemblies positioned discreetly between the beams. Adjustable fixtures on the underside of each assembly target the artwork, while uplights illuminate the Southern yellow pine ceilings to generate a warm and buttery glow inside and out.

Daylight illuminates the dining bridge and gallery bridge as it filters through the continuous glass walls and bands of integrated skylights. Two freestanding rooms in the center of the gallery bridge offer protected spaces to display artwork, with a translucent ceiling membrane diffusing the daylight to meet conservation requirements.

Crystal Bridges opened on November 11, 2011. A large expansion is currently underway. Organized around a second holding pond and new outdoor areas, it will provide more gallery, education, and community space. Safdie Architects and Lam Partners once again teamed up to develop the lighting scheme and continue the immersive experience of architecture, art, and nature.

The pavilions circulate around and over a stream, with the rounded roofs and curving wood ceilings that echo the rolling landscape.

Artwork in the bridge gallery is displayed in two freestanding rooms, with a translucent ceiling membrane to diffuse the daylight.

Sketch detail of the gallery electric lighting and daylighting integration.

There are two lighting assemblies integrated between each beam in the pavilion ceilings. Each curved metal lighting assembly has a track on the underside with adjustable fixtures to target the artwork, and uplights on the top to illuminate the wood ceilings.

Lam Partners The Many Ways of Light

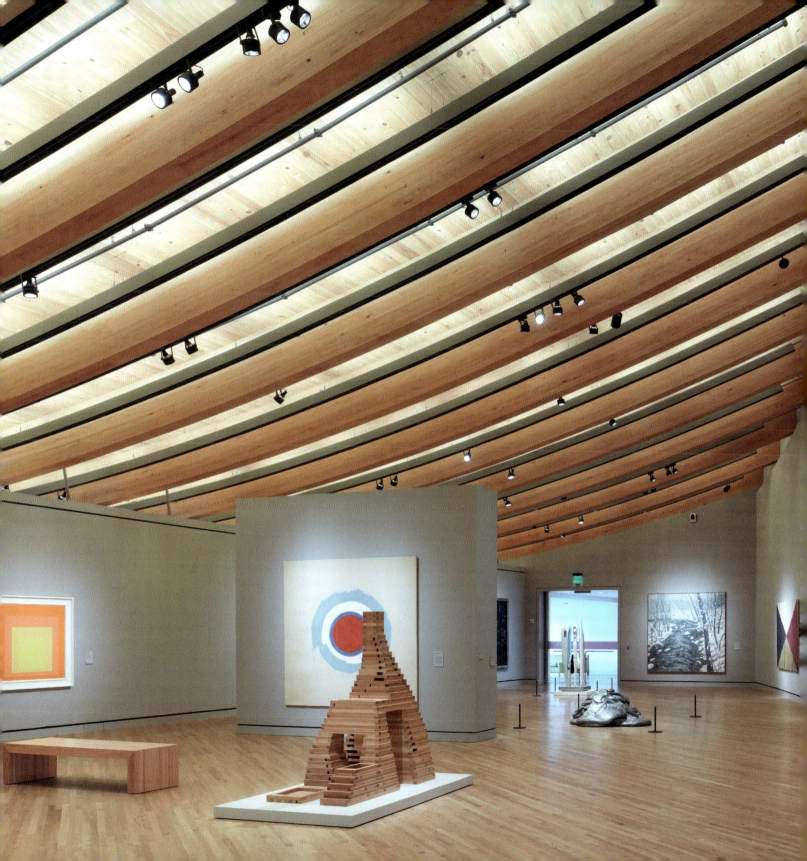

"The sequence of circulation provides visitors with an immersive art experience in the galleries. Then, moving through transition spaces with views out to nature and water, the visitor is recharged, enhancing the overall art experience."

David L. Lawrence Convention Center

Pittsburgh, Pennsylvania

David L. Lawrence Convention Center is a perfect marriage of daylighting and electric lighting, creating a wonderful dialogue that captures Rafael Viñoly Architects' vision. Woven through the building, the two light sources give continuity and expression to the architecture and a seamless transition from day to night.

Rafael Viñoly's vision for a memorable day-lit convention center was a departure from the typical black-box exhibition halls seen throughout the United States. As a structural expressionist, he drew inspiration from the historic bridges spanning the Allegheny River and designed a suspended roof system that made a naturally lit, column-free exhibition hall possible. Lam worked with Viñoly to control the amount of daylight filtering into the convention center and to carefully integrate electric light to work harmoniously with the structure.

Strip skylights on the contoured roof admit direct sunlight and a translucent fabric membrane on the curved southern wall diffuses daylight, both of which interact to animate the grand hall. An active system of shading devices—coined a "solar dimmer" by Lam—can be adjusted to refine the levels and quality of daylight. The motorized system pairs a diffusing translucent shade and a blackout shade that can be unfurled separately or together to create a variety of solar manipulations, from full sunlight exposure to complete blackout.

Electric lighting is discreetly threaded between the mechanical and structural systems to reinforce the arching lines of the exhibition hall. Photocell-controlled linear light fixtures are concealed along the lower structural cables and between paired fabric ducts. These continuous lines of fixtures provide uplight, downlight, and diffused lateral light, creating a soft, shadowless pillow of lighting that illuminates the floor and exhibitions, as well as the soaring architecture.

At night, the ceiling illuminates the public rooftop pedestrian accessway, carved like a canyon through the middle of the convention center. Without any visible sources, the hall glows like a lantern, and the light augments the architecture and expresses its energy.

David L. Lawrence Convention Center was the world's first LEED Gold-certified convention center (now recertified as LEED Platinum) and marked a new chapter for Pittsburgh's reinvention from industrial city to green city.

The illuminated ceiling lights the public rooftop pedestrian accessway without any visible light sources or glare.

Custom hoops help maintain the shape of the fabric ducts when not pressurized, so they can serve as giant diffusers and help baffle the light fixtures from sight.

Fabric shades act as "solar dimmers" on the curved glazing, combining translucent and opaque shades to manipulate daylight conditions.

The linear lighting is not only more energy efficient, but more sustainable than point sources typically used at the time to illuminate expansive volumes.

"Thoughtful architecture is easy to light. It tells us what it wants, and this building very clearly gave us the answer. The lighting is truly in perfect alignment with the architect's vision, and was carefully baked into the entire process."

Phipps Conservatory and Botanical Gardens

Pittsburgh, Pennsylvania

Established in 1893, Phipps Conservatory has long been a sanctuary for Pittsburgh citizens to find pleasure and inspiration amid the botanical gardens. For more than 125 years, Phipps has become one of America's greenest public gardens and a leader in sustainable architecture and operations. Our relationship started with Phipps in 2005 at the beginning of its green revolution, working with the conservatory to integrate modern, sustainable lighting, and to reveal the beauty of the Victorian architecture and plants within.

Helping Phipps achieve its sustainability mission, an incremental series of environmentally responsible improvements made to the conservatory lighting systems have reduced Phipps's carbon emissions. Lighting hardware is replaced only when necessary in order to reduce waste, and the latest technology installed for better energy efficiency and to provide visitors with a memorable experience.

This experience is enriched with the layering of light that illuminates the plants and heritage architecture of the conservatory. Landscape lighting embedded in the gardens focuses on trees, plants, and paths, and track fixtures provide both general lighting and accents on key features throughout the galleries. Uplights around the perimeter walls illuminate the glasshouse ceiling, with the light catching the white steel ribs and glass panels to create the sense of a lit sky above.

Our partnership with Phipps Conservatory over the years has always been about using light to help shape and craft the visual experience of its exhibits and architecture. In 2009, Phipps and glass sculptor Hans Godo Fräbel transformed the gardens into a botanical wonderland with the exhibition "Life in the Gardens: Fräbel Glass at Phipps." The lighting was designed to animate Fräbel's magical glass creations with a sense of life and wonder. The geometric frame glistened and mirrored the surroundings as light bounced across the smooth crystal glass. The pure white quality of the sculptural Longfellows luminesced as they danced in the foliage and across the ponds.

In preparation for its 125th anniversary in 2018, Phipps restored the historic ogee crest structure crowning the Palm Court conservatory. The lighting scheme reveals the complex curves of the original Lord & Burnham design, and color-changing LEDs enable Phipps to celebrate different occasions, transforming the ogee into a colorful lantern for special events throughout the year.

Over the course of our partnership, Lam has guided Phipps from old lighting technologies to new LED technologies and control systems, and worked with Phipps to light the conservatories for special exhibitions and events.

Lighting animated glass sculptor Hans Godo Fräbel's creations in the exhibition "Life in the Gardens: Fräbel Glass at Phipps."

Accent lighting in the landscape requires good color rendering, beam control, and a flexible system that can be adjusted in the same way as lighting in galleries respond to changing art exhibits.

The light brings out the pure white quality of Fräbel's magical glass creations.

"The incremental upgrades are a rolling philosophy of how to make continuous improvements to achieve Phipps's sustainability mission."

The Palm Court ogee crest structure has multiple layers of lighting that enable a rainbow of illumination to slowly move around the dome.

Phipps Conservatory and Botanical Gardens

United States Institute of Peace

Washington, D.C.

The United States Institute of Peace (USIP) is a non-profit organization dedicated to building a more peaceful, inclusive world. Located adjacent to the National Mall, USIP's headquarters is a memorable symbol of peace with an arching white roof that radiates the vibrant energy from within. As the interior lighting illuminates the translucent white roof, it reveals the unique architectural form.

Safdie Architects designed USIP to express transparency and openness with three office blocks organized around two shared atria and capped with a sculptural luminous roof, arching downward like the wings of a dove at rest. The roof is a multilayer system composed of a white outer-glass shell and inner-white fabric membrane sandwiching the steel structure. By day, sunlight transforms the roof into a beautiful umbrella of light that serves as ambient illumination for the atria. In the evening, the glow from within is bright enough for the building to have presence within the surrounding context without detracting from the adjacent memorials and monuments on the Mall.

Achieving this effect without any visible fixtures was a technical feat. Extensive computer modeling, material sample testing, and a full-scale mockup in Germany helped determine the necessary fixture optics required, and the transmissive and diffusing characteristics of the roof to validate the lighting solution. A double row of fixtures placed along the tops of the atria walls illuminates the underside of the roof with a uniform glow. These asymmetric uplights subtly accentuate the curvature of the roof and are dimmed to control the brightness of the exterior surface. The roof overhang is illuminated with ground recessed uplights in the exterior plaza, with the intensity and color matching the interior light for a continuous effect.

The uplighting on the roof provides a comfortable level of ambient illumination in the atria. Supplementing this with downlighting, a discreet line of small adjustable spotlights sparkle along the top of the uppermost window frames, appearing like a delicate necklace within an otherwise hardware-free luminous environment.

Offices fronting the atria make use of the ample daylight. An uplight cove at the back of the offices adds ambient light that spills through a continuous clerestory window, illuminating the central corridors without the need for additional circulation lighting.

The United States Institute of Peace is a masterclass in architectural lighting, embodying Lam's integrated and sustainable lighting principles and supporting Safdie's vision for the building. With fixtures wholly woven into the architecture, it stands calm, transparent, and peaceful by day, and radiates a glowing energy that expresses the landmark at night.

Custom linear pendant downlights in the offices have an asymmetrically deep shield on the window side of the pendant to prevent views of the light source from the atria.

A double row of dimmable fixtures placed along the top of the atria walls uplight the ceiling, and uplights in the exterior plaza illuminate the overhang of the roof to match the intensity and color of the interior light.

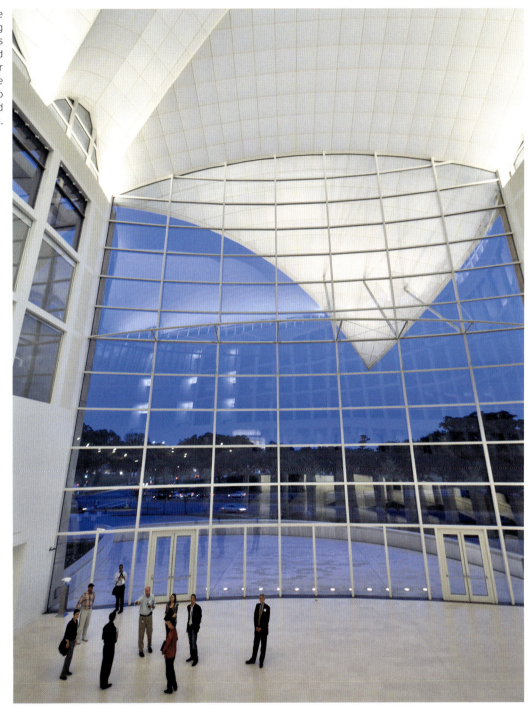

Lam measured the brightness of the existing monuments on the National Mall in order to establish an appropriate level of brightness for the USIP roof.

"This project embodies every principle that Bill Lam established as our core design philosophy. Everything is integrated, with no visible lighting hardware. It's purely luminous architecture."

Boston Public Library Johnson Building

Boston, Massachusetts

Formerly an inward-facing fortress, the Johnson Building at Boston Public Library (BPL) is now a light and vibrant space that opens to the streetscape. The transformation, designed by William Rawn Associates, signifies the changing role of the library and the needs of the community, and the lighting complements the lively new character to welcome, engage, and provide different spaces for visitors of all ages.

The Johnson Building was reimagined in a "New & Novel" way, just as the sign in the lobby reads. The entrance to the library is a large urban room (known as Boylston Hall), featuring a café, radio broadcast studio, and book-shaped pendant lights hanging in the windows as whimsical accessories. Portable book displays are outfitted with concealed lighting that can be plugged into floor receptacles, enabling easy movement and reconfiguration. Overhead, the undulating ribbed ceiling structure adds rhythm and texture, with an integrated light source grazing the wood to create a warm ambience. Recessed LED downlights are used for general illumination and special events.

A central skylight fills the main reading room on the second floor with daylight. A series of distinct rooms around this atrium are represented with different bold colors in the carpet and finishes. Lighting enhances the character and experience of each space, with layers of ambient and task lighting so patrons can find their favorite locations based on comfort and visual needs.

Custom green desk lights on reading tables evoke the traditional fixtures from the historic BPL reading room next door, while large opalescent pendant globes imbue the fiction area and Children's Library with an airy, uplifting atmosphere. A herringbone pattern of linear lights set on the diagonal ensures the bookstacks are well lit in any configuration, providing flexibility for future use. This playful arrangement animates the stack area, with the lines of light suggesting a sense of movement.

With more fun and informality than a traditional library, the Johnson Building brims with life as the engaging design and amenities attract visitors of all ages and backgrounds. The lighting strategies and architectural touches inject energy and vibrancy into the library, creating a dynamic civic center for the community to gather, learn, and share.

The Johnson Building was built in 1972, adjacent to the original classical building designed by McKim, Mead & White in 1895. Dark tinted glazing has been replaced with ultra-clear glass, and the long façade of double-height windows allows for greater daylight, views, and connections.

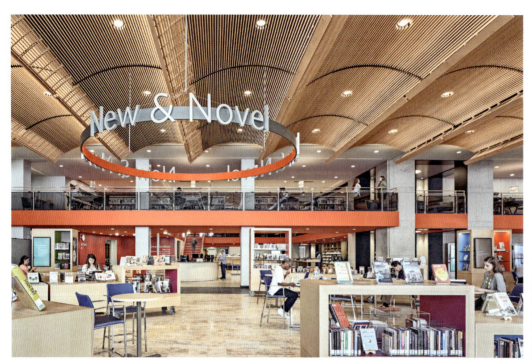

White ceilings with neutral downlights indicate transition zones between spaces in the library.

The ribbed, swooped ceiling structure of Boylston Hall is grazed with concealed linear LED strips. Recessed downlights carved into the wood slats provide general illumination for the various functions within the lobby.

The architect designed a series of different modular bookcases on casters capable of being moved and reconfigured as needed. Integrated lighting is plugged into floor receptacles that are concealed when not in use.

Lam Partners   50   The Many Ways of Light

The pendant direct/indirect fixtures suspended from red ceilings provide general lighting, with softer indirect light to bring out the ceiling color without affecting the color rendering of people and objects.

Lighting is used as wayfinding, with an elliptical ceiling cove over the reading tables, and a herringbone pattern of linear lights above the bookstacks.

"The lighting integrated with the playful, colorful ceiling systems animate the varied spaces of the library, and provide refreshing environments for learning, working, and meeting."

The double-height and arched windows allow for greater natural light to enter the building.

Main Street Station

Richmond, Virginia

Richmond's historical Main Street Station train shed is illuminated with one simple grand gesture: lighting the timber ceiling to create a glow that brightens the event space and expresses the structural form through silhouette. A dynamic layer of color-changing lights adds to the striking effect and ushers in a new chapter for this restored building.

Built in 1901 and designated as a National Historic Landmark, the train shed is one of the country's few remaining with a gable roof, using the same riveted steel frame construction that made skyscrapers possible. The train shed was closed in the 1970s, later restored as a shopping mall, then converted to state offices, and now repurposed into a premium event venue. To revitalize the building, SMBW Architects pared the train shed back to its original riveted steel structure, reskinned it with glass curtain walls, and added a new wood plank roof.

The lighting scheme celebrates the beauty of this architecture with indirect light and limited visible hardware. Fixtures mounted to every truss send light up to the ceiling, transforming it into the primary source of illumination. Custom-sized segmented coves conceal the fixtures on each truss, with additional baffling to mask them from view where the trusses curve down toward the street. The glow of the wood ceiling accentuates the train shed's black steel frame and intricate construction. Downlight fixtures provide additional illumination on the floor, and together the full lighting scheme offers maximum flexibility for use and saving energy.

Vibrant color-changing lights fill the train shed with a celebratory spirit suitable for its new function. Internally illuminated columns mark the edge of the exterior platform on the event level, and fixtures concealed on the lowest flange of the roof truss light the roof overhang. Completing the visual composition, a continuous linear cove fixture located in the roof monitor stitches the entire building together with a colorful beacon running its entire length.

Crafting a new visual expression for Richmond's landmark train shed, the lighting, structure, and detailing work in harmony to shine a light on the beauty of the steel and glass architecture.

The roof overhang is illuminated with color-changing lights concealed on the bottom flange of the truss at the northern end.

Box columns around and within the space are illuminated internally.

The glass curtain walls allow daylight to permeate the event spaces and offer views from inside and outside of the building.

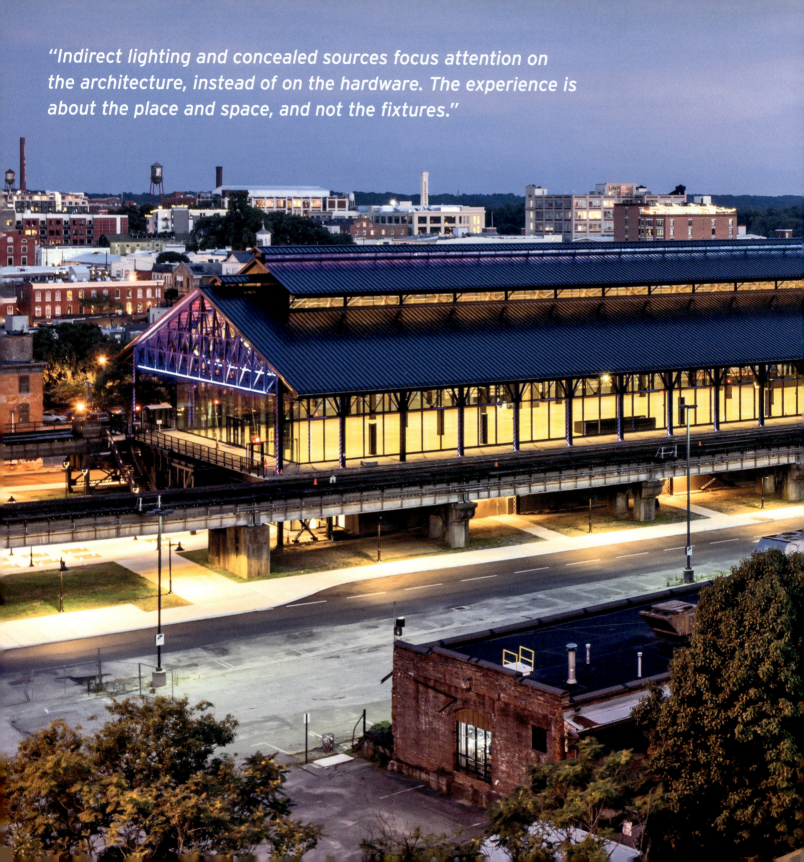

"Indirect lighting and concealed sources focus attention on the architecture, instead of on the hardware. The experience is about the place and space, and not the fixtures."

International Law Office

Boston, Massachusetts

Finely detailed and beautifully appointed, this international law firm office reflects success and instills confidence in its clients. Elkus Manfredi Architects distilled the culture of the firm into the design of its workplace, creating a fresh, modern environment that maintains a sense of heritage and tradition. Working closely with the design team, Lam developed discreet lighting solutions to highlight the intricate details of the interior architecture and the firm's extensive art collection. All fixtures are positioned and aligned so architectural details and artwork are illuminated with museum-quality precision, limiting incidental lighting on other surfaces.

The minimalist and elegant client reception area sets the tone for the office. Luxurious white marble and richly crafted millwork is embellished with brass trim and lacquer panels. Fixtures integrated into the delicate knife-edge cove illuminate the curved coffer ceiling, emanating a soft and ethereal glow. In the conference center, light spills from behind frosted glass panels to showcase the architectural detailing and subtle contrast between matte and satin finishes, while indirectly lighting the pre-function space.

Recessed adjustable accent fixtures illuminate the artwork curated around all four levels of the office and can accommodate changing art programs. The fixtures also provide ambient light, supplemented with wall washers, to illuminate circulation spaces and conference rooms.

The ceiling becomes the primary light source in the private offices, maintaining the crisp, clean aesthetic. Uplight integrated on top of the millwork provides a comfortable, uniform light that enhances the perceived brightness of the office, and task lighting under the millwork highlights the work surface without visible hardware. This integrated lighting approach brings the office experience to the foreground, with fixtures completely concealed by the architecture.

A more playful lighting approach to the cafés adds ornament and sparkle to complement the period-inspired theme. Glowing orbs, wall sconces, and contemporary pendants are decorative accessories that infuse the space with 1930s-style glamor.

The tailored design of this office was achieved by paying attention to and refining every detail. Bright and modern, it maintains the elegance of a traditional law office and conveys the firm's commitment to excellence and expertise.

While traditional private offices in law firms typically use downlighting, uplighting the ceiling provides a uniform and clean aesthetic that blends seamlessly with daylighting.

Artwork accent lighting and concealed linear sources in gathering spaces and conference rooms work together to enhance the overall perception of brightness.

Light through frosted windows at the internal café creates the illusion of being connected to daylight while the interplay between light and material add texture and visual interest to the space.

Light spills out from behind frosted glass panels to showcase the architectural detail and subtle contrast between the all-white finishes.

"With the precision of the architectural detailing and the integrated lighting, the elegance of the office space and the refined material palette is on display for visiting clients as much as the curated art itself. The sophisticated reception lobby immediately welcomes visitors to an elevated law firm experience."

Qaumajuq— Inuit Art Centre, Winnipeg Art Gallery

Winnipeg, Canada

Large and monolithic, Qaumajuq–Inuit Art Centre appears like an iceberg separating from its glacial shelf, its scalloped white stone façade coming to rest over the streetscape at the south end of the Winnipeg Art Gallery. Michael Maltzan Architecture designed Qaumajuq (meaning "it is bright, it is lit" in Inuktitut) in collaboration with Cibinel Architecture and with extensive consultation from the Indigenous Advisory Circle. The gallery houses the largest public collection of contemporary Inuit art in the world, and the interior and lighting provide a space that echoes the atmospheric qualities of Canada's arctic region, where much of the art is made.

The three-story amoeba-shaped Visible Vault is a glistening jewel case of Inuit artifacts. It takes center stage in the lobby and is a conduit between the below-grade conservation department and the light-filled gallery above. Continuous lines of micro track run vertically at the edge of each shelf bay inside the vault, accenting the artifacts without reflecting light in the curved glass enclosure.

Qilak ("sky" in Inuktitut) is the voluminous main gallery, more than 8,000 square feet in size. Evoking the natural environment of the North, Qilak has soaring, sculptural walls and 22 conical skylights that suffuse the gallery with natural light. As the northern light tinges the cavities of the skylights, the gallery is infused with an ethereal blue glow.

Extensive daylighting studies informed the size, shape, and placement of the skylights to ensure the preservation and integrity of the artworks displayed. Each skylight has a light well below, transitioning to a flared opening at the ceiling plane. Removable shade membranes can be applied to further diffuse daylight or close it off completely, if desired. Linear runs of track lighting and mechanical diffusers are laid out on the ceiling to create a graphic pattern radiating from the circular skylights.

The placement and selection of lighting hardware for Qaumajuq, combined with controlled daylighting, helps illuminate the stories of the Inuit people, land, and culture while shaping the galleries with light.

The main gallery has 22 conical skylights that suffuse the sculptural space with natural light. A graphic pattern of track lighting and mechanical diffusers radiates from the circular skylights.

Each skylight has a light well and deep funnel below. Removable shade membranes at the top of the funnel can also be applied to diffuse the daylight or provide blackout conditions.

The optics and distribution for each of the fixtures was carefully selected to wash the large walls in the Qilak gallery and properly focus light on the exhibits, accounting for a broad range of size, type, and material produced by Inuit artists.

Ultra-low-brightness linear downlights on the ceiling and soffit eliminate reflections on the glass lobby and glass vault.

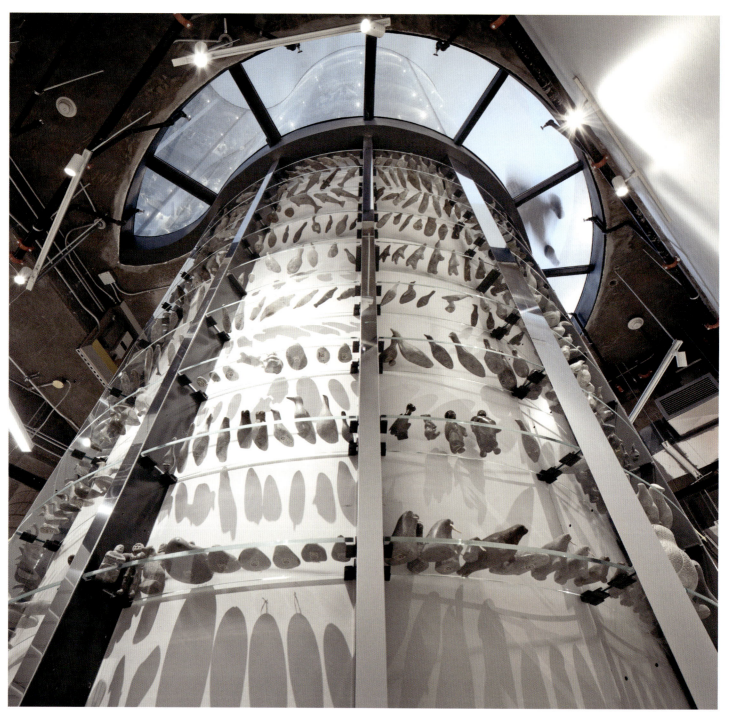

The Visible Vault descends through the glass floor to the archive room below the lobby.

The Visible Vault sparkles inside the lobby, with continuous lines of micro track running vertically at the edge of each shelf bay inside the vault.

The accent lighting system within the Visible Vault consists of tiny track heads mounted to the sides of the vertical mullions and aimed at the sculpture.

"The metaphor of the building is very consistent throughout. It has a distinctive feeling that reflects the environment and culture of Inuit art and is unified in its expression."

Liberty Mutual Tower

Boston, Massachusetts

Completed in 2013, Liberty Mutual's new world headquarters in Boston's Back Bay is a modern tower designed by CBT Architects to blend with the historic character of its surroundings. A major Boston-based company for more than 100 years, Liberty Mutual outgrew its 1937 building. The new tower is located across the street, linked with a glowing pedestrian skybridge, and speaks to Liberty Mutual's longstanding reputation of civic and social integrity.

The private pedestrian bridge connecting the two buildings is a first for Boston. Designed to be as transparent as possible to downplay its presence, the bridge has a cable suspension structure with clear glass walls and ceiling, and a double-layer frosted glass floor assembly. During the day, the bridge is nearly invisible from the street below. At night, it offers a vibrant contribution, as programmable, color-changing LED fixtures in the glass floor cavity emit luminous and dynamic effects. Interreflections in the glass bridge create a subtle kaleidoscopic effect, resulting in a magical experience for both the private and public realm.

Inside the main lobby, illuminated walls and ceilings impart a warm welcome. Featured limestone walls are washed evenly to showcase their natural color and veining. A full-height etched-glass map is discreetly backlit for a uniform glow, while also front-lit with wall wash fixtures to reveal its etched texture and detail. The map is part of a larger art program installed throughout the main circulation and gathering spaces in the new headquarters.

The curving, fluted crown of the 22-story office tower exudes a subtle glow in the night sky. Linear fixtures tucked at the base of each flute illuminate the chevron details in the crown stonework, creating its distinctive and elegant appearance. A mock-up of a 20-foot-tall section of the crown verified the desired lighting effect, and ensured the colors of the carefully selected architectural materials read as the design team intended.

By highlighting specific materials to inform the space and visual environment, the lighting plays a supporting role to the architecture and user experience. At night, the glowing pedestrian bridge is a vibrant presence for the Back Bay neighborhood, while the crown becomes a new icon in the Boston skyline.

Chevron details in the stonework are illuminated with grazing LED linear fixtures at the base of each regress. The overlap of light provides an even and continuous wash on the cornice.

LED spot uplights animate a series of pilasters at the eighth-floor terrace and accent the setback of the building form.

The uniformly backlit etched-glass map turns the entire wall into a light source for the lobby.

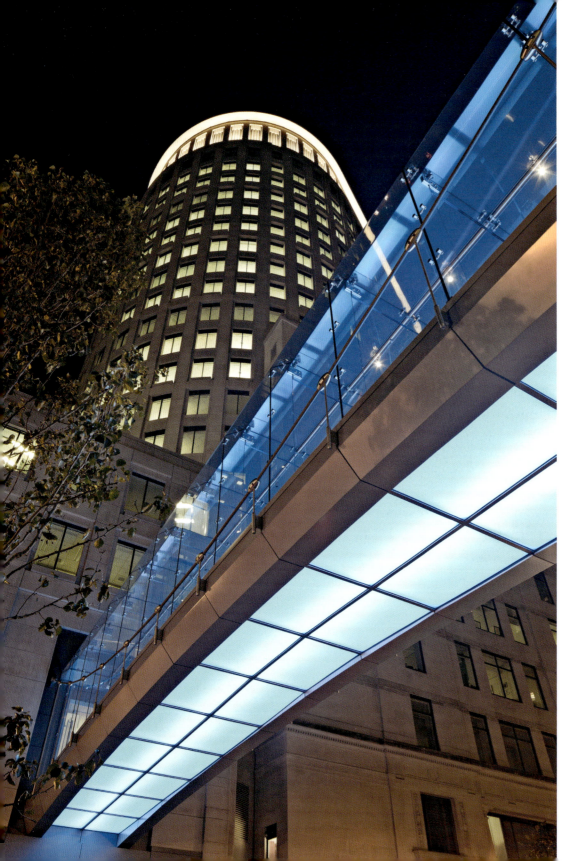

The private pedestrian bridge has a cable suspension structure with clear glass walls and ceiling, and a double-layer frosted glass floor assembly passing over the streetscape as a programmable ribbon of light connecting the buildings and color changing for special occasions.

Numerous photometrically accurate computer models were run in-house to explore different glass properties, testing and visualizing the interaction between light and material, resulting in the wonderful lighted visual experience of the bridge below.

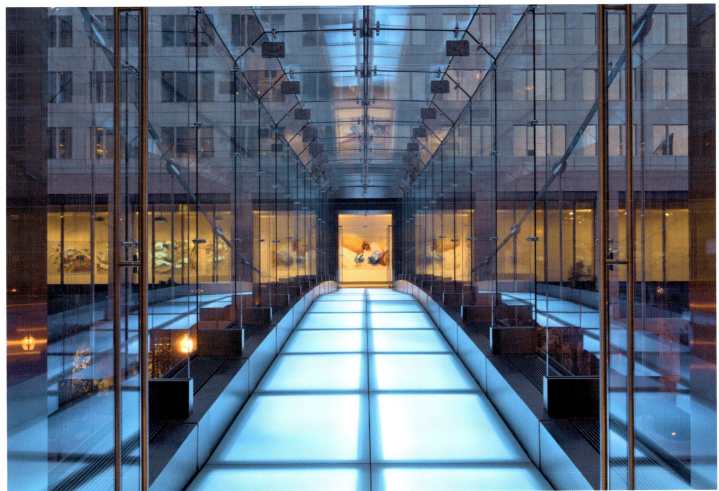

"Liberty Mutual Tower is a signature building within the Boston skyline. The effect is soft and subtle, creating the illusion that the stone cornice itself is glowing."

Concealed exterior fixtures enhance the form of the building massing, and accentuate the building crown.

Dickies Arena
Fort Worth, Texas

The art deco buildings around Fort Worth have a unique Texas flavor reflecting the region's cowboy culture. David M. Schwarz Architects, Inc. continued this tradition in the new Dickies Arena, where every element is intricately detailed and crafted to express this Southwest art deco style. Lam developed custom-designed lighting fixtures to complement the theme, with integrated and decorative lighting to accent spaces and unify the vast entertainment venue.

Elevated on a landscaped plaza, Dickies Arena is a 715,000-square-foot multipurpose facility with a 14,000-seat stadium for sporting events, concerts, conferences, trade shows, and rodeos. Outside the arena, custom octagonal lanterns line the pathways and pedestrian bridge drawing patrons to the spectacular glass entrances on all four sides of the building. The entrance doors are flanked with the same octagonal lanterns, while pole-mounted spotlights enliven the mosaic murals and bronze sculptures around the crown. Lighting illuminates the stair towers from within, emanating a glow through the vertical grilled windows.

The desert rose of Texas became a motif for the decorative lighting throughout the arena, inspiring a star-shaped form conceived in different variations. Rose-inspired lanterns anchor the corners at the top of each tower, and pendants are suspended at the apex of the stairwell and in the lobbies. Fluted wall sconces and ceiling mounted fixtures are used in areas with lower ceilings.

The lobbies are grand, voluminous spaces with marble flooring and mezzanine balconies. The lighting enhances this grandeur, accentuating the architectural form of the ceiling, and adding further art deco flavor. In the North Lobby, custom sconces on surrounding pillars uplight the curvature of the large elliptical convex ceiling, which is reinforced by a perimeter cove that adds to the striking geometry. In the South Lobby, layers of illuminated concentric coves build up to a fan-like display above the mezzanine, and blades of chevron-patterned backlit laylights radiate across the lobby ceiling. Light coves along the sides of the floating ceiling create the presence of daylight.

Further inside the arena, a starfield of decorative glass ball pendants sparkles over the dining tables in the North Club Dining Area, and the bar in the South Club has a distinctive warm glow from backlit onyx stone.

The extensive decorative lighting throughout Dickies Arena reinforces the Southwest art deco theme of the building and landscape for visitors to experience on both a grand and intimate scale. It celebrates the Fort Worth tradition of architecture and the Texas cowboy culture.

Each stair tower has vertical windows with ornamental grillwork and star-shaped lanterns anchoring the four corners.

Uplight from column-mounted custom sconces articulate the large convex ceiling in the North Lobby. The surrounding perimeter light cove floats this ceiling, expressing its distinctive elliptical shape.

The "desert rose" pendant is a signature element at the top of the stair tower. All custom fixtures were coordinated with a manufacturer specializing in traditional, highly detailed work.

Blades of chevron-patterned backlit laylights radiate across the lobby with light coves creating the sense of daylight between the floating ceiling planes.

Site lighting is an integral part of the nighttime arena experience. A freestanding pavilion serves as an internally illuminated lantern on the east terrace. In-grade and ground-stake-mounted uplights highlight the extensive collection of trees throughout.

Many layers of light are all controlled separately to provide maximum flexibility during a multitude of different event types.

Beautiful pendant glass globes add sparkle and ornamentation in the dining area.

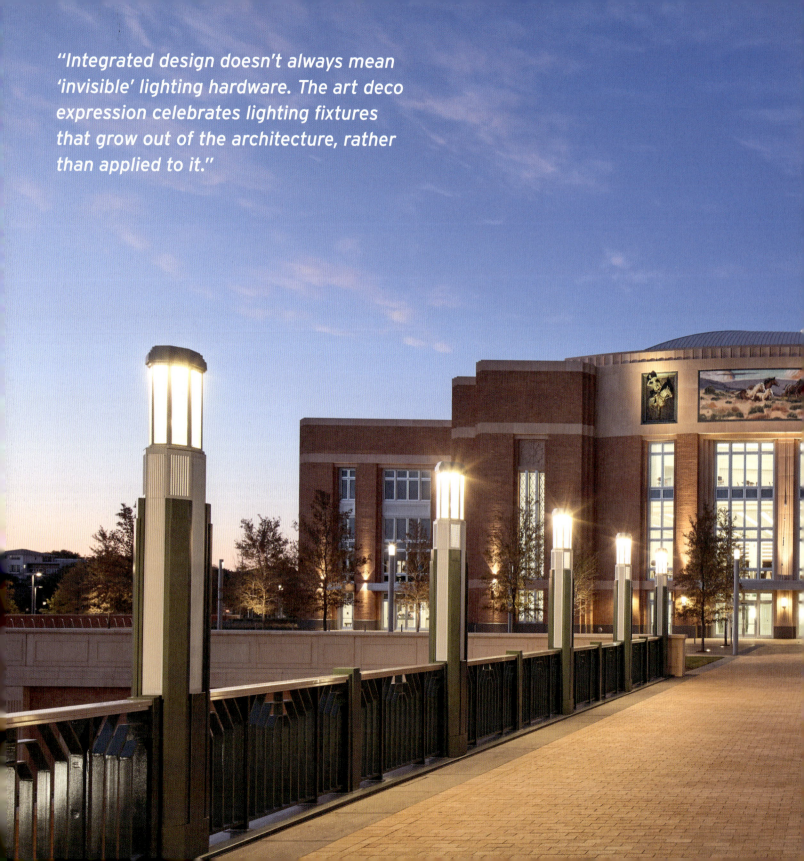

"Integrated design doesn't always mean 'invisible' lighting hardware. The art deco expression celebrates lighting fixtures that grow out of the architecture, rather than applied to it."

Boston City Hall Renovation

Boston, Massachusetts

Boston City Hall has long been a misunderstood building; condemned as one of the "ugliest buildings in Boston," yet revered for being a great architectural achievement. Lam Partners worked with the City Hall Property Management Department and Utile Architecture and Planning to revitalize the original design intent of civic aspiration, connection, and monumentality. Helping to create a safe and welcoming civic heart, the lighting brings the beauty of Boston City Hall out of the shadows and gives vibrant new life to this landmark building.

Kallmann McKinnell & Knowles designed Boston City Hall in the 1960s as part of a major urban redesign, and as a bold example of Brutalist architecture. The openness of the lower levels invited the public to interact with government services, while administrative offices were housed in the cantilevered volumes above. However, over the decades the building was neglected and poorly maintained. Its once grand exterior eroded, and unsightly surface conduit and floodlights attached like barnacles to its underbelly.

Researching the architectural archives of Boston City Hall revealed informative photographs that showed how it was originally lighted. These archival images and the original lighting locations informed the placement and installation of new light sources to reenergize Boston City Hall as Kallmann McKinnell & Knowles originally envisioned—a porous building floating on pilotis. Not only did the lighting strategy pay homage to this vision, but it also paid attention to the intricacies of the structure to emphasize its architectural features.

To float the monolithic building at night, it needed to be illuminated from below. Data and power are sent through existing wires to new color-changing LED fixtures installed in select locations already embedded in the concrete. This indirectly lights the monumental volume and allows Boston City Hall to mark civic events and celebrations with a rainbow of light.

Luminaires are also mounted on city-owned street lighting surrounding the building, with signals beamed via wireless controls synchronizing the color around the building. The wash of light reveals the exquisite craftsmanship of the concrete work and highlights the building's tripartite structure. Additional targeted illumination accentuates the architectural detail and internal programming.

Inside the lobby, each coffer resonates with light. Fixtures are housed in translucent boxes with apertures in the bottom, allowing for direct and diffused light through the depth of the coffer. Together, the lobby and façade lighting create fluidity and transparency through the public realm and elevate the complexity and beauty of the architecture to the level of respect so greatly deserved.

With new LED fixtures, the entire building is lit for a fraction of the watts that the original design required.

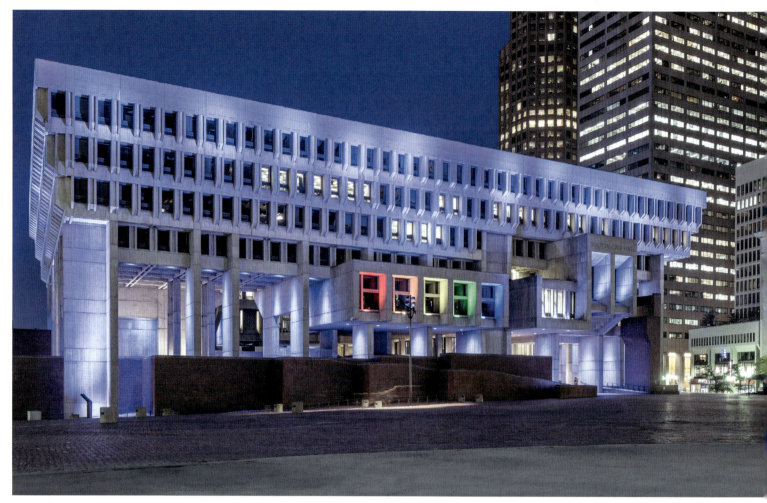

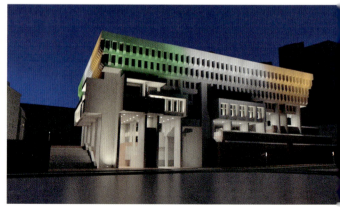

Original large metal fixture housings within each coffer were replaced with translucent acrylic boxes with apertures in the bottom to allow for direct and diffused light.

The lower level of the building is predominantly downlit, but appears to receive uplight by virtue of ground-reflected light (upper left image). In-house computer studies used photometrically accurate lighting visualizations to evaluate possible lighting effects and to finalize fixture aiming specifics (lower row images).

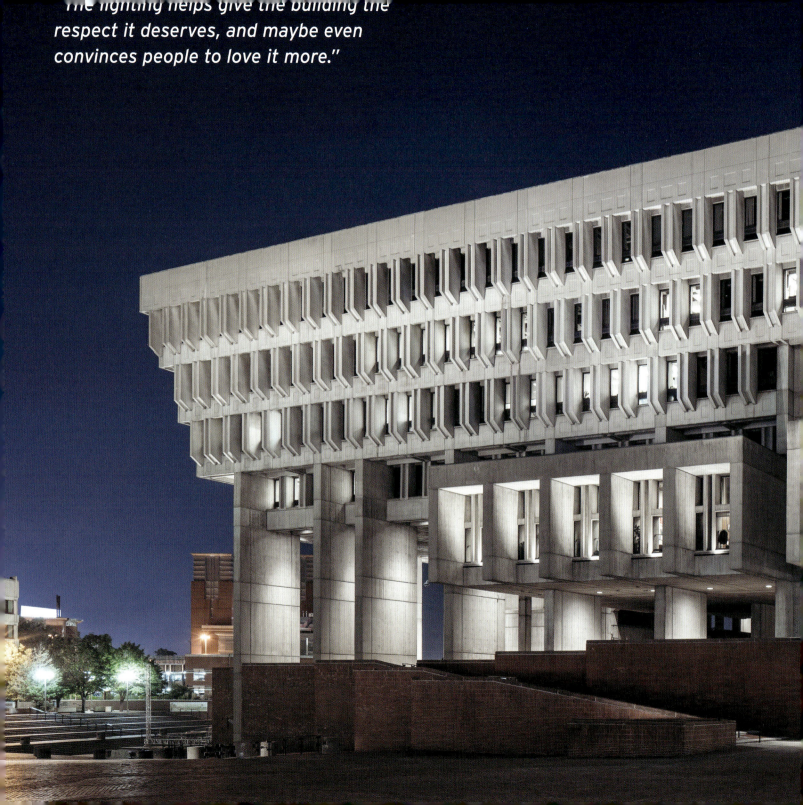

"The lighting helps give the building the respect it deserves, and maybe even convinces people to love it more."

Public Realm

Lighting has a significant impact on how people experience the public realm after dark. Using a variety of lighting techniques, we illuminate outdoor spaces to make them safe, secure, pleasant, and exciting. This selection of projects showcases the ways in which spaces are lit to give them presence and atmosphere with dynamic lighting effects. Establishing a memorable aesthetic and welcoming experience, the lighting encourages public use and contributes to outdoor spaces and amenities that are vibrant and engaging.

Exterior lighting design in some ways is more difficult than interior lighting design. Most every light fixture on an outdoor project is visible from many different vantage points. The assemblage of lighting hardware has to create a visible whole, a hierarchy to create wayfinding and a sense of security. It has to provide an exciting and safe nighttime environment, while being mindful of the night sky and the natural environment. A sensible and targeted approach to exterior lighting leads to better visual environments while preserving the natural environment.

Cambridge Common and Flagstaff Park is the historic center of Cambridge, Massachusetts, and a popular place for locals and tourists to explore and relax. Lam designed the lighting in 1988, and updated it in 2016, improving the illumination along walkways and updating and replacing fixtures with long-life, energy efficient LEDs. The new fixtures reduce glare and energy consumption and dim late at night. The poles also serve as support for accent lighting to give the Civil War monument presence after dark, extending the after-dark hours of park use.

Beyond Walls is a community outreach project engaging the power of art to revitalize and activate public spaces in Lynn, Massachusetts. We partnered with Payette, Port Lighting, and the Beyond Walls non-profit to transform three commuter rail underpasses with visually compelling chromatic lighting. Once unused and avoided, these spaces are now vibrant landmarks where art and light connect downtown and the community, and improve walkability and pedestrian safety.

Cumberland Park is a fun-filled, family-friendly park on the banks of the river in downtown Nashville. Hargreaves Jones transformed the distinctive qualities of the site into opportunities for imaginative play, events, and interactions with the riverfront's industrial history. We integrated lighting to target specific park amenities and features, creating intriguing patterns of illumination across the site. Adjustable fixtures highlight the interwoven meandering paths, and color-changing lights enhance the vibrant, playful atmosphere.

Every summer **Haddad Riverfront Park** in downtown Charleston comes to life with free public concerts, festivals, and celebrations. We worked with Silling Architects to integrate lighting into the band shell and canopies, creating glowing parasols that provide ambient light and visual cues for wayfinding. Dynamic color-changing light can be adjusted to enrich the park atmosphere and performance, and all equipment is submersible as the band shell is susceptible to flood.

Paul L. Foster Campus for Business and Innovation, Baylor University

Waco, Texas

Baylor University opened the Paul L. Foster Campus for Business and Innovation in 2015, providing a vibrant new home for Baylor's Hankamer School of Business. Designed by Overland Partners, the building promotes a progressive twenty-first-century workplace, offering a nexus for a new generation of world-class business thinkers. Lam worked closely with Overland to illuminate the interior volumes in dynamic and inventive ways, shaping the architecture to take advantage of daylight and cutting-edge lighting technology.

Clad in campus-compatible brick on the outside, yet refreshingly contemporary inside, the building has a four-story daylit atrium as the centerpiece of the design. The sculptural atrium ceiling is a grid of deep light wells, inspired by the modular spatial composition of the architectural plan.

This dynamic solution resolved the challenge of bringing daylight into an atrium without glare or thermal discomfort. Each light well is shaped using parametric software to respond to the sun's varying positions, redirecting useful daylight and limiting high-angle direct sunlight. A light scoop above each skylight provides further control, while the orientation of each flared light well allows precise shafts of sunlight to momentarily animate the atrium at certain times of the day and year. This patterning of daylight transforms the ceiling into an active geometric composition of varying brightness as conditions change outside. At night the effect is somewhat reversed, with each light well illuminated by a recessed linear uplight and linear downlights between the light wells. Together they create an abstract weaving reminiscent of the work by textile artist Anni Albers.

Architectural LED lighting hit its stride at the time of this project. Sleek, new 2-inch-wide linear LED fixtures offered a lighting metric that was used to generate a graphic vocabulary of light throughout, also inspired by the work of Albers. The directional quality of this pattern of light reinforced the wayfinding system in the building.

Much of this directional lighting leads to the atrium where the daylight has a vibrant yet delicate quality, evocative of the light in a cathedral. The sky conditions outside inform the perception of space inside, with the shifting beams of sunlight and ambient glow creating an inspiring place to work and study throughout the day.

The stairs are a link between the more traditional architectural style of the campus and the modern, forward-thinking design of this new business school.

The 12-foot-deep roof, housing mechanical equipment and services, provided plenty of depth for the light wells and a catwalk system for maintenance. Recessed uplights are integrated into a cove at the base of each light well and linear downlights line the bottom edges.

Narrow 2-inch-wide linear fixtures offered a new metric that enabled a graphic vocabulary of light throughout.

Each level in the atrium gradually steps back to allow light to penetrate deeper into the lower levels. Cube-shaped rooms cantilevering into the atrium respond to the light well geometry, knitting the interior composition together.

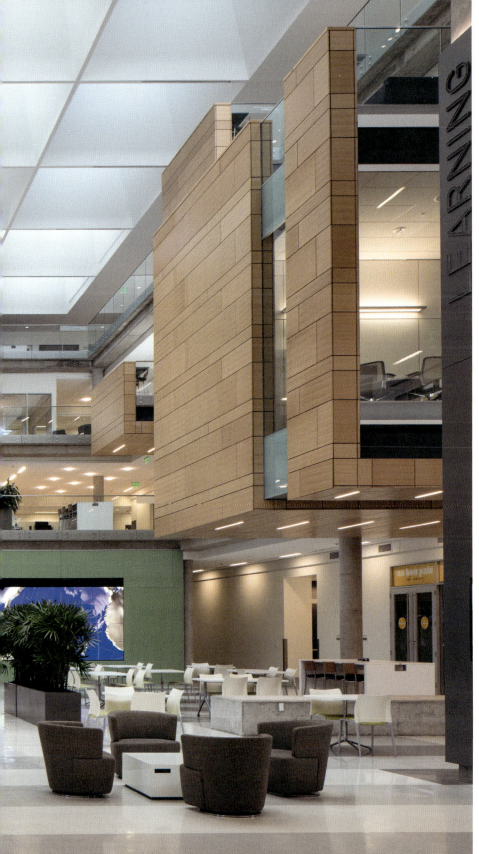

"Each light well appears to have a subtle glow from a distance, but on closer inspection, and from different vantage points, the interplay of light and material creates a dramatic visual experience, providing a unique rhythm and texture to the space."

Each light well is shaped to respond to the sun's varying positions, redirecting useful daylight and limiting high-angle direct sunlight. This patterning of daylight transforms the ceiling into an active geometric composition of varying brightness as conditions change outside.

The National Memorial for Peace and Justice

Montgomery, Alabama

Overlooking downtown Montgomery, the National Memorial for Peace and Justice is a sacred site of remembrance for victims of lynching and terror. A place to reflect on America's history of racial inequality and injustice. Conceived by Bryan Stevenson, founder of Equal Justice Initiative, and developed by MASS Design Group, the memorial is a powerful and evocative site where sculpture, art, and design contextualize racial injustice. Lam collaborated with MASS to cast light on this dark subject and help make it a sobering and meaningful experience.

The memorial presents a forest of 800 Corten steel monuments, each engraved with the name of a state and county, and the names (sometimes "Unknown") of the African American victims lynched in that county. On entering the pavilion, the first rows of monuments rest on the floor. Moving through the pavilion, the wooden deck slopes downward, and the monuments gradually levitate. Each is individually illuminated by a narrow candle-like uplight, pooled below by reflection. As the hollow monuments trap some of the light, a subtle glow is exuded through the stencil-cut inscriptions.

As the floor declines, further monuments are suspended overhead, and a dissolving pattern of uplights creates a dappled, uneven effect. The lights are no longer individually associated with a monument, as if to say, there are too many to count.

Outside the pavilion, each monument has been duplicated and lies on plinths in the memory bank. The Equal Justice Initiative has invited each county to claim and display their monument as part of engaging in the process of acknowledgment and reconciliation. These long narrow plinths are lit from below, producing a continuous glow that makes the monuments above appear to visually float—not resting in place until returned to their respective counties.

Beyond the memory bank lie landscaped spaces for contemplation and discussion. Low levels of light emanating from uplighted trees, low bollards, and softly underlit benches encourage quiet reflection across the reverent site. This carefully and sensitively applied light and shadow heightens the emotion of the memorial and its solemn meaning.

The pavilion is a large square form with an open central court, containing 800 suspended Corten steel monuments inscribed with the names of counties and lynching victims known and unknown.

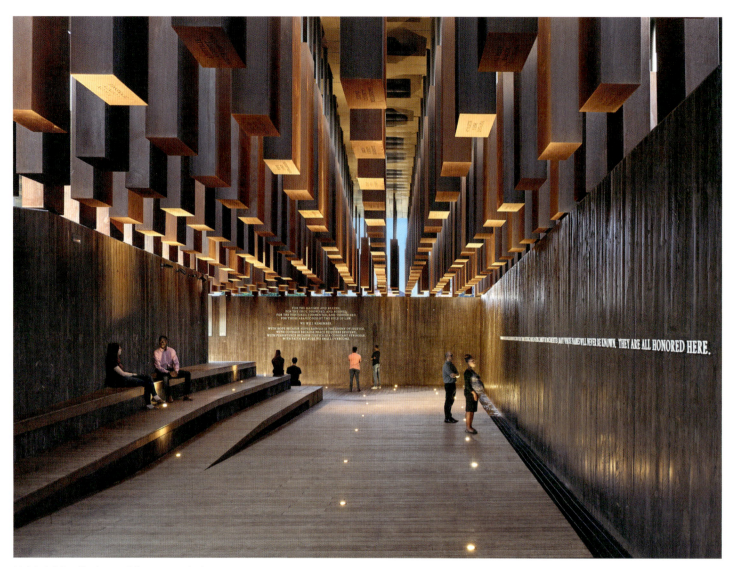

Light striking the base of the suspended monuments illuminates the name of the counties where lynching has taken place.

A dissolving pattern of uplights creates a dappled, uneven effect on the monuments suspended overhead. The subdued lighting reflects the austere atmosphere while meeting minimum light levels for safe passage.

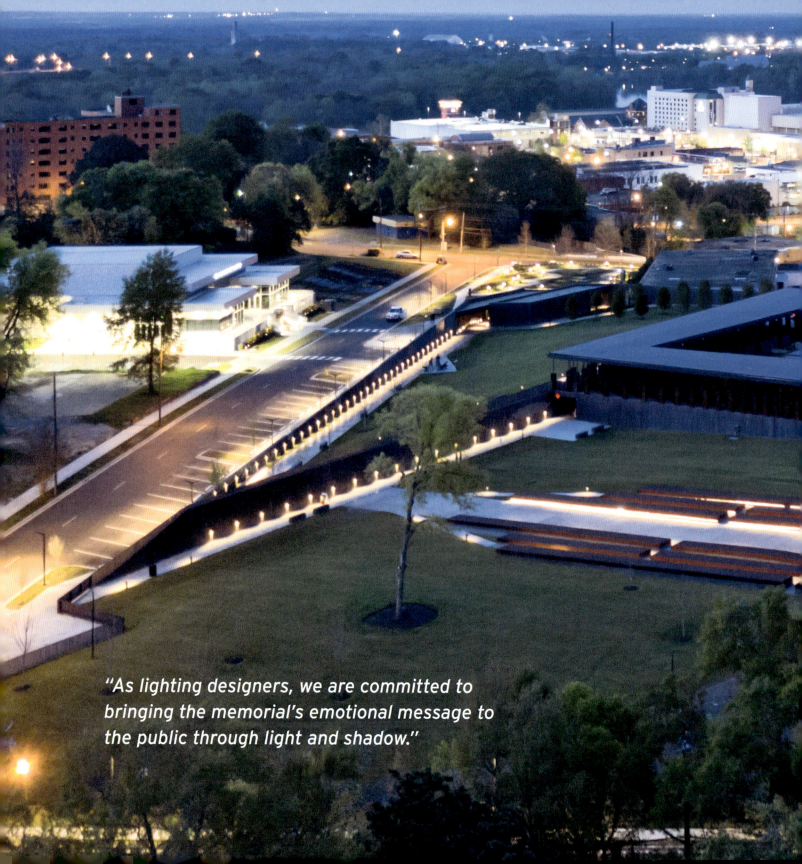

"As lighting designers, we are committed to bringing the memorial's emotional message to the public through light and shadow."

Cleveland Clinic Cancer Institute

Cleveland, Ohio

Natural light is a healing force at the Cleveland Clinic Cancer Institute where access to daylight and outdoor connections help provide a therapeutic environment. William Rawn Associates and Stantec Architecture designed a simple, elongated rectangular building with extensive glass to maximize daylight throughout interior. Layers of direct and indirect electric light supplement the natural light, creating a glare-free environment that complements the elegant simplicity of the architecture.

Cleveland Clinic has a longstanding reputation for clinical excellence and patient care. Its cancer facility is a comforting, professional, and well-organized building that reflects the seriousness and respect their patients deserve. Designed with controlled and considered forms and materials, it has crisp white surfaces and natural stone floors, enlivened with warm wood walls and a contemporary art program.

The patient experience begins at the entry and drop-off area protected by the cantilevered tower above. A long continuous linear LED fixture is integrated on the interior of the glass entry wall and positioned to shine through the glass to highlight the exterior soffit, enlivening the welcoming entryway.

Ceiling and wall lighting helps clarify the overall spatial organization, with fixtures selected for superior glare control and visual comfort. Illuminated white and wood-clad core walls frame the public spaces, while generous coffered ceilings with indirect lighting typically identify waiting areas. Recessed wallwashers and accent lights provide positive focus on the curated works of art, and colorful cove lighting has a calming effect in the MRI rooms.

Patients and staff are never far from daylight and views of landscape. Treatment rooms have generous windows, and glass transoms bring natural light into the interior spaces of the clinical and support areas. Daylight introduced through a large skylight nestled in a landscaped entry island energizes a major circulation passage on the lower floor.

Abundant natural light combined with thoughtfully designed electric light creates a calming and healing environment for patients as they journey through the building and through their treatment. The lighting works with the architecture to craft a sense of welcoming and healing throughout this patient-centric medical facility.

Glare control and ease of maintenance were critical factors in the selection of light fixtures. Numerous samples were acquired for the campus architect and facilities team to evaluate the performance and durability firsthand.

Colorful cove lighting in the MRI rooms provides a calming effect for patients.

Generous coffers are indirectly lit to provide comfortable light over waiting areas. Light slots along the white and wood core walls give order to the architecture and emit a soft glow.

Transoms bring daylight deep into internal spaces.

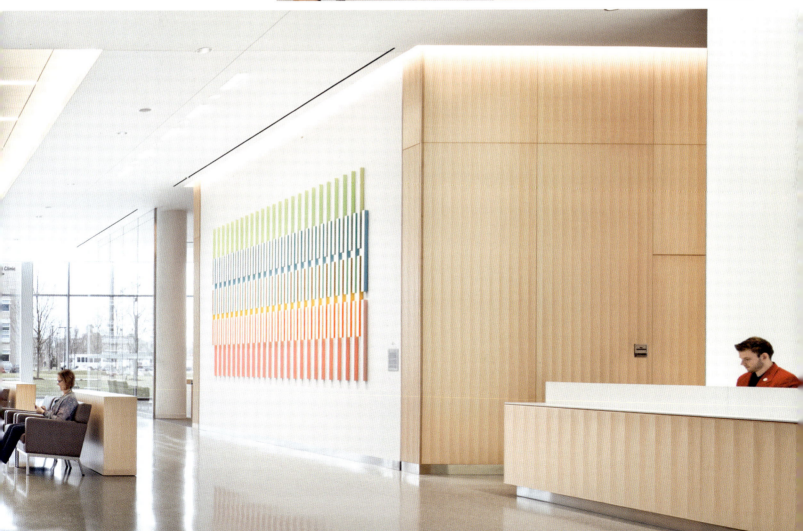

"The building has a great clarity about it and the lighting reflects the honesty of the architecture."

Yad Vashem: The World Holocaust Remembrance Center

Jerusalem, Israel

Yad Vashem, Israel's official memorial to the victims of the Holocaust, is a hallowed site located on the plateau of Mount Herzl (Mount of Remembrance). Safdie Architects crafted a striking and poignant museum symbolically charged with light as a metaphor for hope. Preserving the character of this delicate site, the subterranean museum is a long concrete circulation spine (prism) that pierces the mountain like a spike, revealed only at the ends. A linear ridge skylight capping the prism is the only visible element in the landscape above. The controlled and solemn sequence of spaces within the prism is a moving experience that guides visitors from the dark into the light.

Daylight through the prism skylight becomes a dynamic element in the choreographed path through the museum. It softly washes the sloping concrete walls and casts a beam of light down its length at midday. Deep trenches in the floor—filled with Holocaust Survivors' books, shoes, and other possessions—force visitors to serpentine through the sequence of chapters (exhibit galleries), moving slowly toward the light at the end of the prism, where the cantilevered terrace splays out to overlook Jerusalem Forest.

At night, the skylight is a softly glowing line in the landscape. Narrow-beam spotlights beneath flush glass panels in the floor light the top of the steep concrete walls so the skylight appears to glow. With no visible light sources or hardware to detract from the deeply moving subject matter, the visitor experience remains focused on the emotion and content of the museum.

Holocaust victims are memorialized in the Hall of Names. A skylight above a suspended conical form brings daylight in to illuminate photos displayed inside the cone and provides ambient light to the space surrounding it. A glimmering light in the depths of a reciprocal cone penetrating into the earth commemorates those victims with names unknown.

Yad Vashem is a deeply emotional and moving experience, with the powerful content and meaning captured by the architect. With Safdie's use of light as a metaphor for hope and the endurance of the human spirit, Yad Vashem is visually striking and simply unforgettable.

Visitors exit the museum through a beautiful, quiet courtyard where they can contemplate and reflect on the experience.

Daylight studies determined the appropriate light levels that maintain the solemn feeling without inhibiting the preservation of the exhibits and objects below.

A skylight above a suspended conical structure creates a funnel of light to illuminate photos and the surrounding space. A cove uplight, concealed in the cone base perimeter, takes over when daylight wanes.

"The lighting is purposely subdued. You see and feel the presence of light and the ambient illumination around you, but the sources are downplayed. It reinforces the solemnity of the place and experience."

Narrow-beam spotlights illuminate the top of the steep concrete walls so the skylight appears to glow.

MIT Media Lab, Massachusetts Institute of Technology

Cambridge, Massachusetts

Maki & Associates' addition to the existing MIT Media Lab marked a fresh era of innovation for the interdisciplinary research groups exploring advanced technologies for the enhancement of human life. Orderly, detailed, and purposeful, the building is full of magic, creativity, and surprises, much like the research performed within it.

Fumihiko Maki designed the six-story building with high levels of transparency through the interior and exterior. Single and double-height labs are organized around an upper and lower atrium with a skylit winter garden on the top floor. Daylight from the central skylight is suffused down through the atria by way of fabric screen laylights and glass floors. Glass walls surrounding the atria offer unobstructed views into the labs from multiple interior levels. These transparent and translucent volumes combine like giant interwoven LEGO® blocks to promote dynamic connections between people and their research.

The lighting system heightens the activity and movement in the building. Uplights in the elevator pits illuminate the bottom of the elevator cabs as they ascend and descend. Marker lights embedded into the floors and stair treads create synaptic-like sparkle with the movement of people as they crisscross the large spatial volumes. Lighting meticulously integrated into cavities, cored openings, and coves help to highlight the forms and materials of the building with little exposed lighting hardware.

Enhancing the sense of display in the laboratories, data-enabled track lighting systems are individually controlled and focused on events and experiments. These systems provide the flexibility to create different scenes and atmospheres, while carefully tailoring the light to the programmatic needs of the laboratory.

This exterior glazing is veiled with a tubular brise-soleil to control solar gain and selectively frame the laboratory blocks. Based on daylight conditions, the laboratories remain visually opaque during the day. At night the interiors of the labs and atria come alive, and the building becomes a lantern revealing the energy from within.

A visionary building designed for revolutionary research, MIT Media Lab provides an inspiring environment for collaboration and invention. Lighting promotes the transparency of space and form to expose the creative science and ignite wonder and excitement for the research taking place within.

The laylight is indirectly illuminated with uplights concealed in round apertures cored into the wall. The hole-in-the-wall design is also used to conceal a framing projector that invisibly projects large images on the opposite two-story wall.

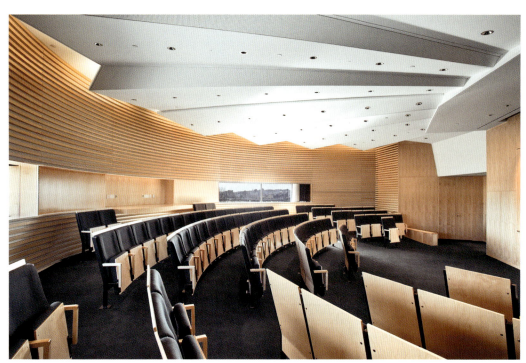

Lighting emphasizes the warmth of the wood and expresses the folds of the origami-like ceiling in the upper round lecture hall.

Laboratories double as technology exhibits. Multi-zoned track lighting and dimming controls provide the flexibility to program and tailor different lighting moods and scenes.

Electric lighting concealed in cavities, cores, and coves highlight interior surfaces and extends the sense of daylight deep into the atria. The undersides of the elevator cabs are illuminated with spotlights in the elevator pits.

"The transparency of the building celebrates the movement and creativity within, like the synapses of the brain firing across multi-level laboratories and atria."

Laboratories are organized around an upper and lower atrium with a winter garden on the top floor. A tubular brise-soleil veils exterior glazing to control solar gain and selectively frame the laboratory blocks.

Salt Lake City Public Library

Salt Lake City, Utah

Visitors to Salt Lake City Public Library enjoy soft, controlled daylight entering the building from every direction. This thoughtful approach to natural light results from Safdie Architects' masterful building parti. Conceived with light as a metaphor for enlightenment, the architectural forms of the library are shaped with the intent to create spaces with useful daylight and views to the surrounding site and mountains beyond. Lam collaborated with the architectural team to achieve a seamless daylighting and electric lighting design.

The building is composed of simple and familiar geometric volumes, oriented to maximize access to daylight throughout the library. At the center of the composition, the triangular-shaped main library block houses the bookstacks and readers' facilities. A continuous light well buffering the afternoon sun links the administration wing to this block on the west side. Sweeping around the east side, a crescent-shaped wall ramps upward from the south plaza and rises to the full height of the triangular library. A great "urban room" is captured between the library triangle and the crescent wall, drawing the public in, promoting interaction, and hosting civic functions.

A five-story double-glazed "lens" on the southeast side of the triangular library block is a strategic part of the thermal management and lighting design. In summer, this buffer zone protects the library from direct sun and incorporates a vent system at the top and bottom for cooling air flow. In winter, the lens stores heat, while sunlight passes through to brighten the library beyond. A rippling sea of canvas shades at the bottom of the lens filters light into the children's room below.

Indicative of Safdie's level of refinement, the development of custom light fixtures adheres to his affinity for clear and simple geometric forms. Linear pendant uplights in the library block are derived from the segment of a circle and illuminate the shallow ceiling vaults to provide uniform, glare-free illumination throughout.

During the day, the north-facing windows of the crescent wall, together with the skylight in the urban room to the south, fill the reading area with balanced daylight. In the evening, custom scoop-shaped uplight fixtures illuminate the ceiling for general lighting. Specially designed linear table-mounted fixtures are used for additional task lighting. Lantern-like fixtures mounted on the columns in the urban room continue the pedestrian path through the space and provide a human scale to this soaring volume.

With light, openness, and transparency forming the library's DNA, the allegory of enlightenment is beautifully expressed in the inscription across the three glass elevators: "People who live/in glass houses/shall throw no stones."

The "lens" allows low-angle winter sun into the library for natural light and warmth while shielding high-angle summer sun to reduce glare and heat gain. Canvas shades soften sunlight into the children's room below.

Lantern-like fixtures mounted on the columns in the urban room continue the pedestrian path through the great "urban room."

The building arrangement maximizes access to natural light, and celebrates openness and transparency.

Frosted glass panels bookend the stacks with backlit printed library information.

"Salt Lake City Public Library is a thoughtfully conceived and executed public building, fulfilling its vision of what a great library should be."

Visible through the glazing, a raised floor system contains all the mechanical, electrical, and data systems, keeping the ceilings clear for indirect lighting.

Guggenheim Bilbao Museum

Bilbao, Spain

Fluid architectural forms with a sense of movement and energy set a new precedent for the relationship between architecture and art in Gehry Partners' Guggenheim Bilbao Museum. The colossal titanium-clad building, with interior volumes that push and pull at the building's envelope, required a lighting strategy that provides appropriate artwork illumination without compromising the expressive spirit of the building. Frank Gehry's break from traditional gallery design led to the development of a new lighting system in response to his approach.

The primary purpose of museum lighting is to satisfy a full range of exhibition requirements, which includes understanding proper aiming angles and art conservation needs. That presented two major challenges for this museum: First, the need to control daylight. Second, how to incorporate a flexible art lighting system into the complex geometric forms.

Skylights within each gallery are angled and sculpted to control the amount of daylight in the space, while preventing direct sunlight from reaching the artwork and walls. Motorized fabric shades below the skylights adjust for seasonal variation and to reduce or eliminate daylight based on the sensitivity of an installation.

Testing detailed physical models of the galleries on a heliodon determined the optimum angle, depth, and shape for the light wells, and Sun Scan quantified the daylight in the galleries. This customized computer program developed by Lam Partners normalizes the daylight data received in the models (tested in Santa Monica) for the project-specific latitude and time of year. For the qualitative analysis, a camera secured to the physical models produced detailed videos of light patterns in the galleries from the path of the sun from sunrise to sunset.

The electric lighting system was specifically developed to provide flexibility for lighting artwork without the conventional lines of recessed track permanently scarring the ceilings. A system previously developed by Gehry and Lam for the Weisman Art Museum in Minneapolis was further refined for the Guggenheim. A grid of structural outlet boxes are recessed into the ceiling and concealed with retractable, magnetic cover plates. When in use, track fixtures and additional clamping bars can be integrated into the concealed system to provide the gallery with endless flexibility in fixture locations, positions, and aiming, all while maintaining a clean and pure ceiling aesthetic.

Designing the lighting for the Guggenheim Bilbao Museum was an exploration of new ideas that transformed thinking about art lighting at this scale. This new lighting system satisfies the technical and conservation requirements of the museum and works in unison with the dynamic architectural design to enhance the overall visitor experience.

In the galleries with very high or irregularly shaped ceilings, suspended catwalks hold the lighting equipment and other services in order to facilitate easy access and maintenance. The geometry of the catwalks directly responds to the aiming angle required for artwork illumination, thereby mimicking the various shapes of the galleries and becoming another sculptural element throughout.

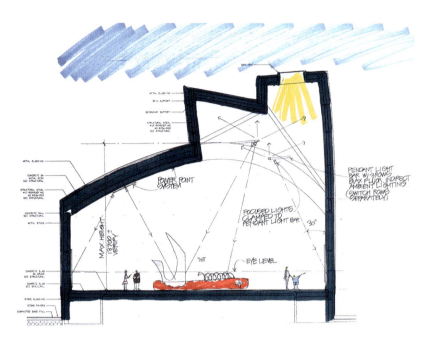

Concept diagram of different natural and electric light sources within a gallery.

When power bars are angled on gallery ceilings in response to specific art installations, their pattern takes on the expression of that particular exhibit. When not in use, retractable magnetic covers on the power points sit flush with the ceiling, rendering them virtually invisible. Any lighting manufacturer's fixtures can be used with the clamping power bar system to accommodate changing technology over the years.

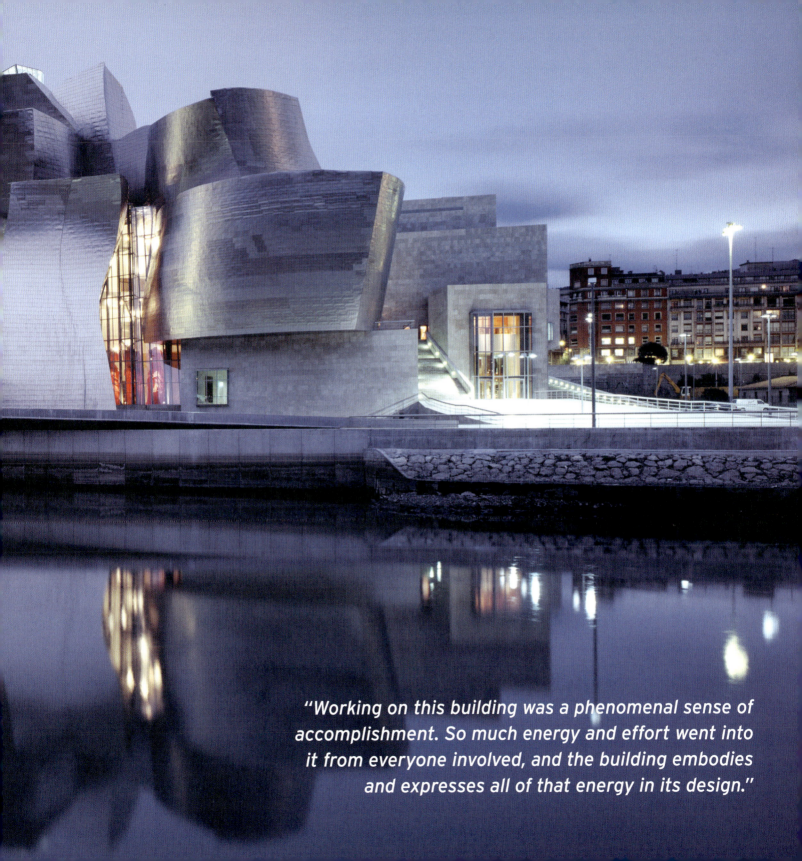

"Working on this building was a phenomenal sense of accomplishment. So much energy and effort went into it from everyone involved, and the building embodies and expresses all of that energy in its design."

Harry Reid International Airport

Las Vegas, Nevada

When Tate Snyder Kimsey Architects (TSK) designed the Satellite D terminal at McCarran Airport in the late 1990s, it wanted to create a destination and gateway that celebrated arrival and departure to and from the thrilling metropolis of Las Vegas. Modern and metallic, the terminal fostered a streamlined visitor experience. Lam collaborated with TSK to integrate creative lighting solutions that complement the elegance and efficiency of the terminal and passenger journey. This architectural and lighting design language has been maintained throughout the terminal expansion over the decades.

The original Satellite D building is predominantly illuminated with concealed indirect electric lighting and redirected sunlight and daylight. A soaring glass curtain wall, offering views of the airfield and city beyond, has architectural light shelves to minimize direct sunlight penetration by redirecting it onto the ceiling. Daylight through clerestory windows transforms the ceiling into a bright and lively light source that draws the eye down the center of the concourse. Long linear pendant light fixtures provide ambient illumination and wayfinding alongside the gates.

TSK expanded Satellite D in the early 2000s to accommodate additional concourses sand gates. Lam employed similar lighting solutions, using architectural light shelves and pendant linear fixtures for discreet lighting and visual continuity.

In 2017, the airport opened a 995-foot-long tunnel below the tarmac for international passengers to transfer from Satellite D to Terminal 3. Lam worked with Gensler to brighten and enliven the subterranean journey. Curving lines of custom light fixtures and contrasting materials create a visual pulse and a sense of direction and movement through the windowless tunnel. This rhythm is generated by a series of polished metal panels with concealed linear fixtures on the backside that are shielded from view of one-way passenger travel. Light grazing the wall and ceiling surfaces fading before the next panel accentuates the contrast between the specular and matte surfaces. This dynamic, futuristic effect is counterbalanced on the opposite wall by a mural illuminated from a long, fully concealed light slot.

In keeping with the original design intent, the tunnel and terminal celebrate passengers' arrival to Las Vegas at the renamed airport by providing a memorable gateway to an exciting tourist experience, while enhancing wayfinding and balancing brightness and contrast ratios to maximize visual comfort.

Skylight monitors deliver daylight over the stairs and escalator that form the entrance to the underground tunnel.

A necklace of light-box cavities brightens the central rotunda with an ambient and ornamental lighting effect.

Daylight through clerestory windows transforms the ceiling into a bright and lively light source. Indirect lighting hidden on the clerestory light shelf recreates the same daylight effect at night.

"The lighting effect completely changes based on your viewing direction. Arriving passengers see softly washed panels as they face forward but turning around reveals a texture of lighted ribbons."

Austin United States Courthouse

Austin, Texas

Courthouses are often considered austere public buildings with little public appeal. Mack Scogin Merrill Elam Architects, Inc. wanted to dispel this notion of the traditional courthouse. Instead, it envisioned the Austin United States Courthouse as a light-filled, welcoming building for the public to enjoy while still asserting civic strength and pride.

The glass façade provides this modern monolithic building with a sense of transparency, bringing daylight into the interior and offering passers-by a view of a mural by renowned American artist Clifford Ross. The architects commissioned the glass wall artwork as a vibrant focal point, separating the lobby from the jury assembly room beyond.

Lam collaborated with Ross to determine how to best light his artwork. Printed onto film and sandwiched between two glass panes, it needed to be uniformly lit form both sides. Extensive testing of daylight variables and electric lighting strategies was performed to ensure no color degradation over time. Concealed lights at the base of the glass and recessed lighting at the ceiling, on both sides of the artwork, accentuate the brilliant colors, enlivening the lobby and adjacent plaza and park. This lighting is balanced with uniform illumination throughout the lobby to support security requirements and give the building a warm, inviting night presence.

Daylight enters all seven stories of the building through glazed fissures within the limestone massing. Luminous ceiling panels mimic a sense of daylight in the wood-paneled courtrooms, blurring the lines between electric light and daylight. They are supplemented by perimeter illumination to enhance the spatial brightness of the courtroom.

Lights concealed in architectural pockets illuminate materials and highlight internal volumes. The slipped planes and deconstructed massing of the building allows light energy to escape from the core and emanate from the envelope. This lighting throughout Austin United States Courthouse reinforces its transparency and reaffirms the architect's vison of a courthouse as a civic oasis rather than a fortress of security.

The modular design of the backlit ceiling provides a unifying ornamental feature for the courtroom. Accessible ceiling panels at the edges of this feature make it easy to maintain.

Inspired by Austin's Hill Country, Clifford Ross's The Austin Wall is a composition of glass rectangles in vibrant colors that creates a dramatic abstraction of sky, water, earth, and foliage. The lower portion features a panoramic black-and-white image of the local landscape, based on Ross's photograph.

Miniature custom baffles were detailed to conceal the hardware lighting the artwork, minimizing source brightness so not to distract from the illuminated glass feature wall.

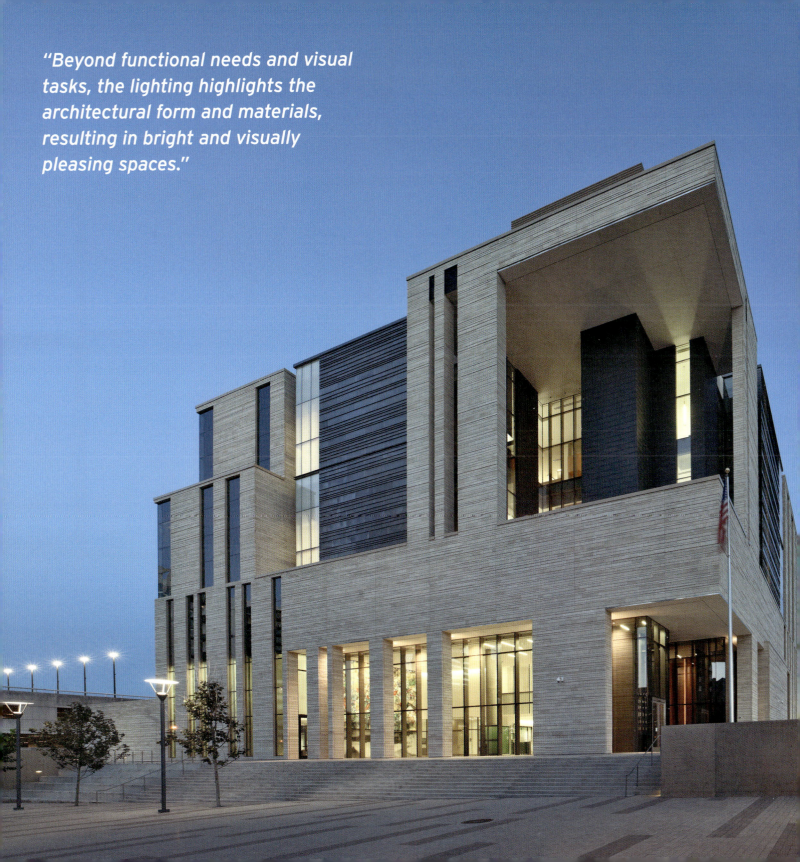

"Beyond functional needs and visual tasks, the lighting highlights the architectural form and materials, resulting in bright and visually pleasing spaces."

Free Library of Philadelphia

Philadelphia, Pennsylvania

Libraries have evolved in the digital era. No longer simply repositories of books, they provide valuable spaces and services for the community. Safdie Architects' renovation of Free Library of Philadelphia's Parkway Central Library transformed six levels of dark, cramped bookstacks into three levels of bright and welcoming public spaces for the library of the twenty-first century.

Safdie's vision for a "trellis" ceiling brings together the decorative coffered ceilings in the historic main entrance hall and reading room of the 1920s beaux-arts building with the checkered pattern on the tiled floor. This vision was expressed in a grand gesture with a continuous pattern spanning the rooms of the library, suggesting it has always existed.

The trellis ceiling comprises 1,400 light fixtures, each with one or two downlights for focus, and an uplight illuminating the ceiling with a soft uniform glow. The custom fixtures appear identical, but there are actually six different lengths to resolve the non-symmetrical spacings between the existing terracotta-clad beams. Independent mud-in flanges on both sides of the fixture are installed into perfectly cut square holes within the drywall surrounding the beams. With no visible connection points, the trellis ceiling appears as one majestic integrated feature. Controllable light levels allow for flexibility between day, night, and evening events.

The Field Teen Center takes on a different character, with large round coves carved out of the dropped ceiling showcasing the existing columns and beams. Fixtures around the interior shelf of the coves indirectly light the space for glare-free ambient illumination on young library users' screens.

The grand scale of this lighting and ceiling required a truly collaborative effort between Lam, the architects, contractors, and manufacturers. The result is an integrated system that fits seamlessly with the architecture and complements the grandeur of the historic library.

Large backlit panels mimic windows on internal rooms, creating a perceived connection to natural light and the outdoors.

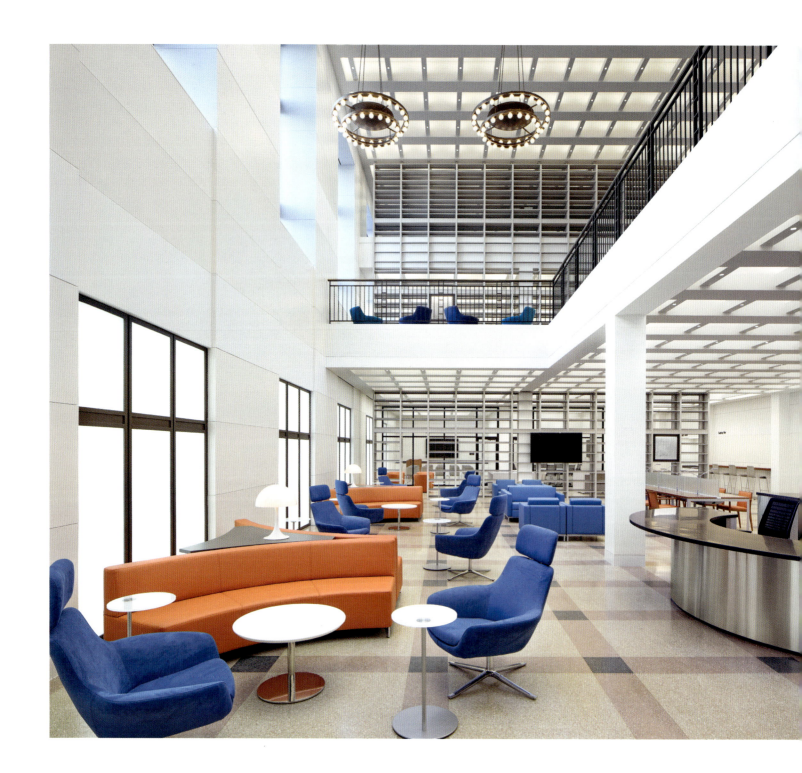

Custom chandeliers nod to the beaux-arts architecture of the library, with dimmable LED lamps allowing for different light levels.

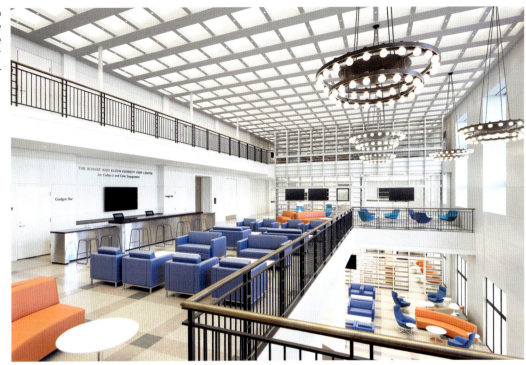

Concealed coves in the Field Teen Center provide indirect ambient light that enhances the volume of the ceiling coffers while providing glare-free comfort for library users.

The 3-foot-on-center spacing of the fixtures aligns with the steel structure replicating the historic bookstacks.

"As a public amenity for the City of Philadelphia, it's wonderful to see people enjoying the library and having it so well received. Lighting was an integral piece in the transformation of this civic space."

The Tower at PNC Plaza

Pittsburgh, Pennsylvania

The Tower at PNC Plaza in Pittsburgh is a landmark building with high aspirations driven by PNC's strong workplace, environmental, and social values. These include the desire to create an office that holistically addresses user experience, sustainable performance, and a contribution to the urban area. Lam collaborated with Gensler to achieve PNC's ambitious challenge to design "the greenest skyrise in the world." This lofty goal required innovative daylight and electric lighting solutions that balanced form and function, human and operational needs, and longevity and efficiency.

The 32-story tower is positioned to take advantage of daylight and views, with workstations oriented perpendicular to the façade on all sides of the building. This reduced the need for electric light during the day but posed the challenge of how to maximize daylight penetration and minimize solar glare for a comfortable work environment.

Working closely with Gensler, a window blind and lighting control system was developed that prevents glare and heat gain from direct sunlight. The blinds are sandwiched within a cavity of the double-skin glass façade and programmed to articulate throughout the day based on solar position. The sequence of operation balances daylight and brightness with the quality of the visual environment, while a control system enables PNC to adjust the blinds to optimize energy use and worker experience.

The orange core of the building is wrapped with a custom continuous perimeter light source to help balance the incoming daylight at the façade. As the core light radiates from the interior and daylight filters in from the exterior, they blend seamlessly to create balanced illumination across each floor. The core light dims at night while all other lights are turned off, reducing energy use, providing sufficient illumination for security, and bestowing the building with a subtle orange glow.

The Tower at PNC has earned Platinum LEED certification and set a new standard for energy efficiency and sustainability. This sustainability extends beyond environmental performance to elevate the workplace environment and experience, and to support and contribute to the development and growth of downtown Pittsburgh, serving as a symbol of PNC's commitment to the city's sustainable future.

The shading system within the double-skin glass façade is programmed to articulate throughout the day to prevent glare and heat gain.

Elliptical ceiling coves in the cafeteria mimic the shape of the serveries beneath them.

Daylight and electric light blend seamlessly to create balanced illumination across each floor.

The Tower at PNC Plaza operates using half the energy of a conventional office building of equivalent size.

The circular lighting is inspired by the curved form at the west end of the building that cleverly joins the intersection of areas.

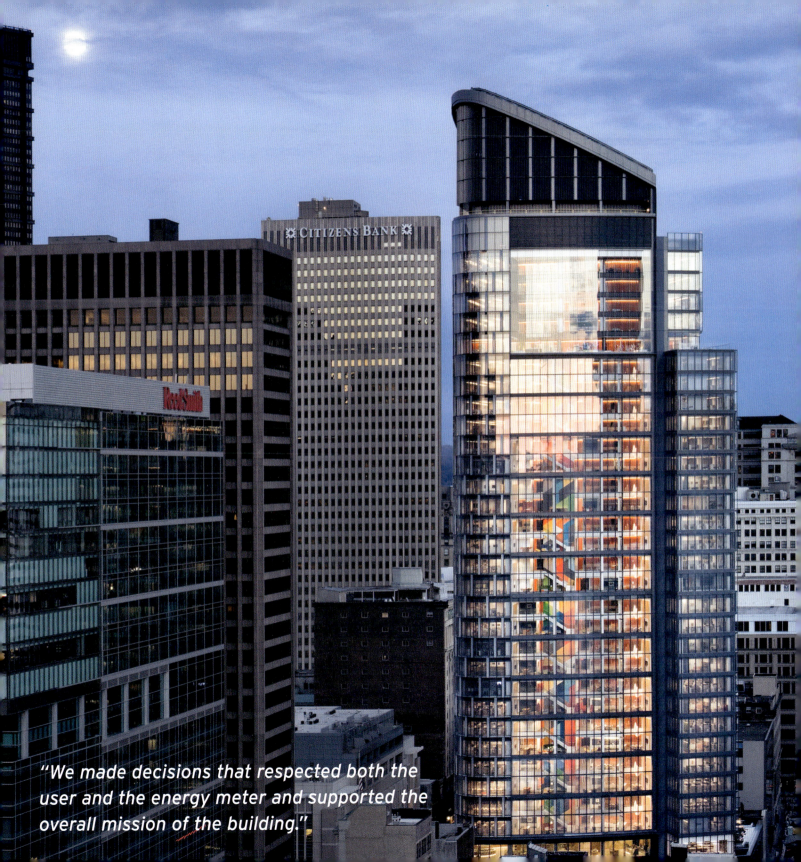

"We made decisions that respected both the user and the energy meter and supported the overall mission of the building."

New World Center

Miami Beach, Florida

Unlike many of Frank Gehry's other notable buildings, New World Center is like an architectural geode: a simple form on the outside, but rich with color, texture, and angular shapes on the inside. Designed by Gehry Partners for Michael Tilson Thomas's New World Symphony, the building is a dynamic architectural setting where sound, vision, and light are explored and experienced together.

Gehry designed the simple white exterior to reference the white stucco and art deco buildings characteristic of Miami Beach. The large rectangular building is organized in three parts: a bar building at the south end for administrative functions and practice rooms, a large central atrium with three levels of rehearsal and multipurpose rooms, and the concert hall at the north end of the site.

A wave-like canopy marks the entrance into the atrium where daylight pours through the large central skylight and soaring glass curtain walls. A series of stacked sculptural volumes enclose practice spaces and ensemble rooms. This composition of "music boxes" is a dramatic collision of forms, with glazed wedges between the boxes allowing daylight and views into each. Continuous rows of aimable fixtures mounted beneath the skylight and along the glass walls at multiple elevations illuminate the atrium at night. Washed with white or color-changing light, the boxes appear to float when viewed from outside. Integral step lights animate the curving stair, and a backlit color-changing glass bar with a blue titanium canopy anchors a gathering space between performances.

From the atrium, concertgoers pass through a softly lit serpentine corridor to reach the performance hall, where they are immersed in Tilson Thomas's imaginative world of music and vision. Seating unfurls around the stage, while five billowing acoustical sails above reflect sound and provide projection surfaces to enhance the performance with a visual experience.

Adjustable fixtures discreetly clustered and concealed in ceiling panels between the sails and central floating cloud are carefully aimed to wash the seats and aisles with light, while avoiding spill-light on the sails themselves. A color-changing cove encircles the ceiling cloud and can be programmed with the projection on the sails or provide a soft glow over the stage.

An overhead skylight and large north-facing window bring natural light into the performance hall during the day. Outside the window, ground-recessed fixtures illuminate a large architectural sunshade designed to appear like an interior curtain blown outside by the breeze—another great gesture by Gehry to the Miami Beach setting. Like all of New World Center, light, material, and form work harmoniously to create a vibrant place to enjoy sound and rhythm.

The central ceiling cloud, containing remotely controlled theatrical fixtures, is rimmed with a color-changing LED cove that can be programmed with the projection on the sails or to simply provide a soft glow over the stage.

Lam Partners **172** The Many Ways of Light

Adjustable fixtures are discreetly clustered between the acoustical sails. These fixtures are carefully aimed then locked in place to light the seats and aisles, while avoiding spill-light on the sails.

The stacked volumes in the atrium take on a sculptural, floating character as they are washed with light. The public can enjoy performances projected on the exterior of the building, and the roof garden features a large terrace for special events.

"The practice spaces and ensemble rooms are playfully stacked and sculpted with a collection of windows facing the curtain wall and atrium, giving the public a peek into the activity inside. The organization is simple and brilliant, visionary and imaginative."

SoFi Stadium

Inglewood, California

Extraordinary architecture often requires an extraordinary level of ingenuity and technology across all divisions to make a project shine. SoFi Stadium—a unique indoor-outdoor stadium and the NFL's largest—was a remarkable feat of design, engineering, and construction. Working with HKS Architects on an accelerated design and construction schedule, Lam developed the lighting design for all public-facing areas of the stadium and the entire 60-acre site and surrounding landscape, as well as the colossal color-changing LED media mesh system on the top of the roof.

To develop the lighting for SoFi Stadium, Lam built a high-performance, in-house rendering farm to model and simulate the lighting design in real time, responding to changes and developments in the complex architectural geometry during the design phases. Using this high-performance rendering and parametric modeling, iterations of lighting models could be quickly adapted despite the scale and schedule of the project. The workflow technology developed for SoFi Stadium is now used in a majority of projects, advancing Lam's modeling and visualization capabilities.

The ethylene tetrafluoroethylene (ETFE) roof canopy is a translucent stretched fabric panelized system that provides clear sky views, while also shading spectators below. LED fixtures concealed behind large structural girders around the edge of the perforated metal canopy wash the underside of the roof structure with colored light and accentuate its form arching over the stadium. Rivulets of light cast through the perforations create a rich play of light, shadow, and texture, and a dynamic lantern effect at night. The building skin becomes an organic and vibrant element that pulses with changing lighting, creating a diaphanous connection to the stadium energy within.

Additional façade lighting provides illumination where the roof meets the ground, altering the apparent opacity of the metal skin from day to night and from one location to another. As ingrade lighting washes up the large blade columns around the edge of the canopy, it defines a monumentally prominent outer edge to the building, enhancing the structure and beauty of the architecture.

A custom-designed 35,000-pixel LED media mesh system draped across the entire clear membrane turns the roof into a one-of-a-kind translucent video screen. Passengers flying into LAX at night can see the roof transformed into a giant video billboard for advertising and live-action game footage.

Combining the lighting, architecture, and embedded video technology makes SoFi Stadium an exciting and memorable visual experience unlike any other sporting venue in the world.

The playing surface within the bowl of SoFi Stadium sits 100 feet below-grade to meet FAA regulations in building height restrictions. Entering the stadium from the surrounding site, at the main concourse level, presents a view and an arrival experience unlike any other NFL stadium.

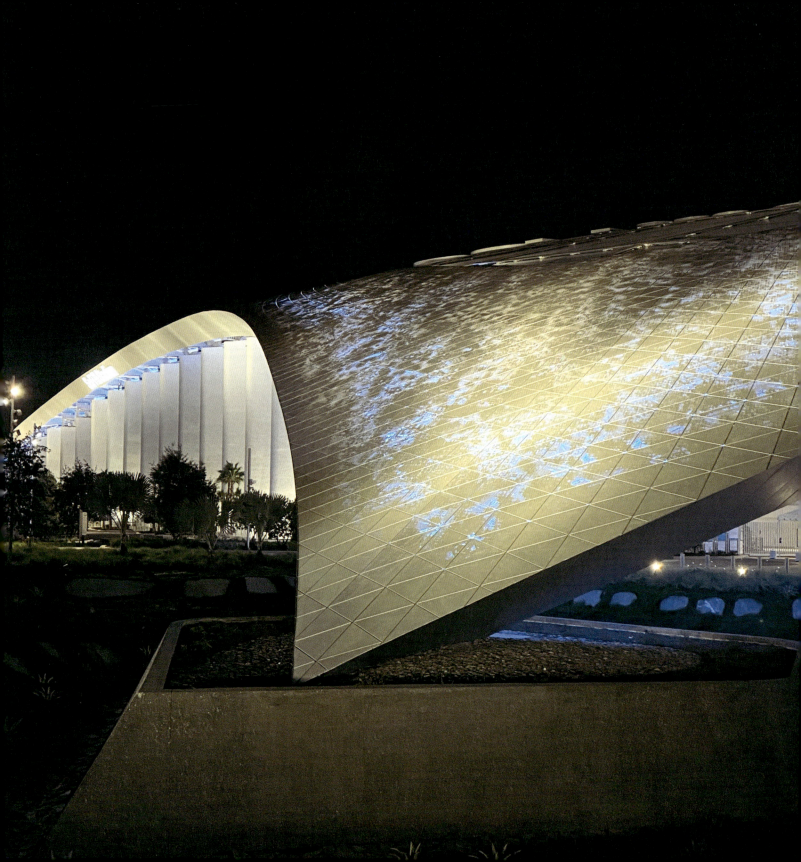

Passengers flying into LAX at night can see the stadium and the roof transformed into a giant video billboard. Computer models rendered thousands of light fixtures to accurately simulate the aerial visual experience seen from planes overhead.

Illuminated columns in the distance, give the open-air structure the sense of enclosure from certain views.

The fully programmable, color-changing lighting is an integral part of the stadium nighttime experience, pulsing with the energy and excitement from within.

Ground mounted façade lights wash the roof canopy where it engages the ground plane, while color-changing lighting concealed within the structure filters through the perforated metal skin of the stadium, transforming the opacity from one area to another.

California native plant life and the associated landscape lighting continues from the site down terraced canyons to VIP entries, blurring the lines between interior and exterior spaces.

Daylight creates a dappled effect on the concourse as it filters through the perforated metal façade panels.

The roof also features a series of operable panels distributed around the perimeter of the ETFE to promote air flow throughout the stadium. The ETFE membrane has a frit pattern that provides shading comfort for patrons below while allowing for clear views of the sky above.

"The low, gentle curvature of the roof line masks the sheer size and scale of the footprint of this one-of-a-kind project. The visual experience as you approach the stadium from across the park exemplifies the art and science of painting with light, shaping moods and emotions while creating a sense of space and place."

Acknowledgments

This monograph is a culmination of our 60-plus years in the lighting design business and is a true labor of love for all those who helped capture the story of Lam Partners. Throughout its writing, we were reminded of the many opportunities we have had to be involved with some of the world's most distinguished and impactful projects. It is often said that you can't have great lighting without great architecture. It takes the foresight and commitment of those architects and building owners who understand the importance of a high-quality visual environment to create timeless buildings and great spaces for people.

To all the architects and clients who have given us the opportunity to collaborate on the many amazing projects featured in this book, as well as those not featured, we owe you a debt of gratitude. We are grateful for the relationships we have built over the past 60 years and look forward to the next 60. Thank you for your confidence and making Lam an integral team member in the design process.

Our design staff—past and present—has been the backbone of our firm. Their dedication to design excellence throughout the many ups and downs in the design and construction process has resulted in our best work. Talented individual contributions combine in an amazing synergy making our projects a true collaborative effort; those where the original author is often unknown, and the successful design is shared by all. The collective enthusiasm for what we do and what connects us is a large part of what makes our work together so enjoyable.

Our administrative staff has always been an essential part of Lam's overall success. From business and financial management to marketing, tech support, and running the day-to-day operation of our business, they keep our machine well-oiled and in top shape. Managing a group of designers—"herding cats"—and keeping our business on track is no small feat!

The Images Publishing Group has guided us through this amazing and sometimes laborious process, helping us craft this wonderful retrospective and storytelling of our firm. Our writer and editor, Rebecca Gross, has helped us weave beautiful lighting narratives into the visual presentation of our projects.

Lastly, we would like to acknowledge the tremendous support and patience given by our family members, significant others, and close friends as we have exercised our craft over many wonderful years. Spending more time commenting on the lighting rather than the menu in a restaurant tends to be an occupational hazard to which they have grown accustomed. And for that, and everyone mentioned here, we are very appreciative.

Project credits

Kauffman Center for the Performing Arts
Location: Kansas City, Missouri, USA
Completion: 2011
Client: Kauffman Center for the Performing Arts
Architect: Safdie Architects
Size: 356,000 SF
Photography: Michael Spillers, Glenn Heinmiller

Crystal Bridges Museum of American Art
Location: Bentonville, Arkansas, USA
Completion: 2011
Client: Crystal Bridges Museum
Architect: Safdie Architects
Size: 200,000 SF
Photography: Timothy Hursley
Diagram: Lam Partners

David L. Lawrence Convention Center
Location: Pittsburgh, Pennsylvania, USA
Completion: 2003
Client: Sports & Exhibition Authority of Pittsburgh and Allegheny County
Architect: Rafael Viñoly Architects
Size: 1,486,000 SF
Photography: Brad Feinknopf/OTTO, Stephen Lee

Phipps Conservatory and Botanical Gardens
Location: Pittsburgh, Pennsylvania, USA
Completion: ongoing
Client: Phipps Conservatory
Size: 43,500 SF
Photography: Paul G. Wiegman, c/o Frabel Art Foundation

United States Institute of Peace
Location: Washington, D.C., USA
Completion: 2011
Client: Endowment of the United States Institute of Peace
Architect: Safdie Architects
Size: 154,000 SF
Photography: Bill Fitzpatrick, Glenn Heinmiller

Boston Public Library Johnson Building
Location: Boston, Massachusetts, USA
Completion: 2016
Client: City of Boston
Architect: William Rawn Associates, Architects, Inc.
Size: 156,000 SF
Photography: Bruce T. Martin

Main Street Station
Location: Richmond, Virginia, USA
Completion: 2019
Client: City of Richmond
Architect: SMBW Architects
Size: 100,000 SF
Photography: Matt Latchford, Ansel Olson

International Law Office
Location: Boston, Massachusetts, USA
Completion: 2020
Client: Confidential
Architect: Elkus Manfredi Architects
Size: 216,500 SF
Photography: Connie Zhou

Qaumajuq–Inuit Art Centre, Winnipeg Art Gallery
Location: Winnipeg, Manitoba, Canada
Completion: 2021
Client: Winnipeg Art Gallery
Architects: Michael Maltzan Architecture (design architect), Cibinel Architecture Ltd. (executive architect)
Size: 36,000 SF
Photography: Lindsay Reid

Liberty Mutual Tower
Location: Boston, Massachusetts, USA
Completion: 2010
Client: Liberty Mutual Insurance
Architect: CBT Architects
Size: 900,000 SF
Photography: Robert Benson Photography, Lumenpulse, Richard Mandlekorn

Dickies Arena
Location: Fort Worth, Texas, USA
Completion: 2020
Client: Event Facilities Fort Worth, Inc.
Architects: David M. Schwarz Architects, Inc. (design architect), HKS, Inc. (architect-of-record)
Size: 715,000 SF
Photography: Steve Hall/Hall + Merrick Photographers

Boston City Hall Renovation
Location: Boston, Massachusetts, USA
Completion: 2019
Client: City of Boston
Architect: Utile Architecture and Planning
Size: Lobby 13,800 SF; transaction area 3,800 SF; entire exterior façade
Photography: Anton Grassl

Paul L. Foster Campus for Business and Innovation, Baylor University
Location: Waco, Texas, USA
Completion: 2013
Client: Baylor University
Architect: Overland Partners
Size: 285,000 SF
Photography: Paul Bardagjy

The National Memorial for Peace and Justice
Location: Montgomery, Alabama, USA
Completion: 2018
Client: Equal Justice Initiative
Architect: MASS Design Group
Size: Interior 30,100 SF; exterior 6.5 acres
Photography: Iwan Baan, Alan Karchmer/OTTO, MASS Design Group

Cleveland Clinic Cancer Institute
Location: Cleveland, Ohio, USA
Completion: 2017
Client: Cleveland Clinic
Architect: William Rawn Associates, Architects, Inc., and Stantec Architecture
Size: 337,000 SF
Photography: Robert Benson Photography

Yad Vashem: The World Holocaust Remembrance Center
Location: Jerusalem, Israel
Completion: 2005
Client: Holocaust Martyrs' and Heroes' Remembrance Authority
Architect: Safdie Architects
Size: 191,000 SF
Photography: Timothy Hursley

MIT Media Lab, Massachusetts Institute of Technology
Location: Cambridge, Massachusetts, USA
Completion: 2009
Client: Massachusetts Institute of Technology
Architects: Maki & Associates, Leers Weinzapfel Associates
Size: 163,000 SF
Photography: Anton Grassl/ESTO

Salt Lake City Public Library
Location: Salt Lake City, Utah, USA
Completion: 2003
Client: Salt Lake City Library
Architect: Safdie Architects
Size: 225,000 SF
Photography: Timothy Hursley, Paul Zaferiou

Guggenheim Bilbao Museum
Location: Bilbao, Spain
Completion: 1997
Client: The Guggenheim Museum
Architect: Gehry Partners
Size: 260,000 SF
Photography: David Heald
Diagram: Lam Partners

Harry Reid International Airport Terminal 1
Location: Las Vegas, Nevada, USA
Completion: 1998
Client: Clark County Department of Aviation
Architect: Tate Snyder Kimsey Architects (TSK)
Size: 1,100,000 SF
Photography: Timothy Hursley

Harry Reid International Airport Gate Expansion
Location: Las Vegas, Nevada, USA
Completion: 2017
Client: Clark County Department of Aviation
Architect: Gensler
Size: 29,000 SF
Photography: Ryan Gobuty/Gensler

Austin United States Courthouse
Location: Austin, Texas, USA
Completion: 2012
Client: General Services Administration
Architect: Mack Scogin Merrill Elam Architects, Inc.
Size: 250,000 SF
Photography: Timothy Hursley

Free Library of Philadelphia
Location: Philadelphia, Pennsylvania, USA
Completion: 2019
Client: Free Library of Philadelphia
Architects: Safdie Architects (design architect), Kelly Maiello Architects (architect-of-record)
Size: 45,000 SF
Photography: Michael Bixler, Barry Halkin/Halkin Mason Photography, Lisa Wong, and others courtesy of Free Library of Philadelphia

The Tower at PNC Plaza
Location: Pittsburgh, Pennsylvania, USA
Completion: 2016
Client: PNC Financial Services
Architect: Gensler
Size: 800,000 SF
Photography: Connie Zhou

New World Center
Location: Miami Beach, Florida, USA
Completion: 2011
Client: New World Symphony
Architect: Gehry Partners
Size: 100,000 SF
Photography: Moris Moreno, Claudia Uribe

SoFi Stadium
Location: Inglewood, California, USA
Completion: 2020
Client: StadCo LA, LLC. and Hollywood Park Land Company, LLC.
Architect: HKS, Inc.
Collaborating lighting designer: KGM Lighting (for suites and clubs only)
Size: 3,100,000 SF
Photography: Bruce Damonte, Nic Lehoux

Washington Metropolitan Area Transit Authority Stations
Location: Washington, D.C., USA
Completion: 1976–1990s
Client: Washington Metropolitan Area Transit Authority
Architect: Harry Weese & Associates
Size: System-wide expansion
Photography: Lam Partners

Custom House Tower
Location: Boston, Massachusetts, USA
Completion: 1987, updated 2008
Client: Boston Edison
Height: 496 F
Photography: Lam Partners

Massachusetts State House
Location: Boston, Massachusetts, USA
Completion: 2002
Client: Commonwealth of Massachusetts
Architect: Goody Clancy
Size: 500,000 SF
Photography: Stephen Lee

Washington Union Station
Location: Washington, D.C., USA
Completion: 1988
Client: United States Department of Transportation
Architect: Harry Weese & Associates
Size: 607,000 SF
Photography: Paul Zaferiou

Cambridge Common
Location: Cambridge, Massachusetts, USA
Completion: 2016
Client: City of Cambridge
Architect: Halvorson Design Partnership
Size: 16 acres
Photography: Glenn Heinmiller / Lam Partners

Beyond Walls
Location: Lynn, Massachusetts, USA
Completion: 2018
Client: Beyond Walls Lynn
Architect: Payette
Size: 2 acres
Photography: Warren Jagger

Cumberland Park
Location: Nashville, Tennessee, USA
Completion: 2012
Client: City of Nashville
Architect: Hargreaves Jones
Size: 6.5 acres
Photography: Kenny Clayton Photography

Haddad Riverfront Park
Location: Charleston, West Virginia, USA
Completion: 2010
Client: City of Charleston
Architect: Silling Architects
Size: 3 acres
Photography: Richard S. Lee

Current and past team members

*Lam Partners current team members, at time of publication, are in bold

William M.C. Lam
Anna Baranczak
Jeff Berg
John Birdsey
Molly Bowman
Justin Brown
Maura Clark
Peter Coxe
Niki DeSimini
Nathanael Doak
Olivia Eckard
Sarah Fisher
Susan Gebhardt
Carlene Geraci
Maggie Golden
Chad Groshart
Jim Hamilton
Kourtenay Hanrahan
Glenn Heinmiller
Amber Hepner
Chris Hoyman
Steve Iski
Kelly Jones
Michael Joy
Carla Wille

Jonathan Knickerbocker
Brad Koerner
David Laffitte
Kera Lagios
Dianne Lam
John Lam
Tom Lam
Matt Latchford
Karmen Lee
Suji Lee
Catherine Leskowat
Peter Lew
Will Lewis
John Logiudice
Brittany Lynch
Ken McKelvie
Alicia Miksic
Marietta Millet
Eda Muco
David Nelson
Paul Newsome
Victor Olgyay, Jr.
Robert Osten
James Perry
Dan Pham

Jennifer Pieszak
John Powell
Chris Ripman
Jack Risser
Laura Rohan
Enrique Rojas
Carly Rothbauer
John Rubio
Sara Sahebghalam
Jennifer Sanborn
Amy Stein
Meredith Stoneking
Kevin Sturrock
Srushti Totadri
Ann Tweed
Steph Valencia
Cheryl Wanner
Dan Weissman
Penn Whitlow
Lisa Wong
Wenjin Wu
Keith Yancey
Meg Young
Paul Zaferiou

Published in Australia in 2023 by
The Images Publishing Group Pty Ltd
ABN 89 059 734 431

OFFICES

Australia
Waterman Business Centre
Suite 64, Level 2 UL40
1341 Dandenong Road,
Chadstone, VIC 3148
Australia
Tel: +61 3 8564 8122

United States
6 West 18th Street 4B
New York, NY 10011
United States
Tel: +1 212 645 1111

Shanghai
6F, Building C, 838 Guangji Road
Hongkou District, Shanghai 200434
China
Tel: +86 021 31260822

books@imagespublishing.com
www.imagespublishing.com

Copyright © (text) Rebecca Gross and Lam Partners; photographers as indicated 2023
The Images Publishing Group Reference Number: 1637

All photography is attributed in the project credits on pages 188–190 unless otherwise noted.
Pages 2–3: Nic Lehoux (SoFi Stadium); Page 6: Timothy Hursley (Albert Einstein Education and Research Center); Pages 8–9: Michael Spillers (Kauffman Center for the Performing Arts); Page 9: Timothy Hursley (Crystal Bridges Museum of American Art); Page 12: (clockwise from top left): Lam Partners (Custom House Tower); Stephen Lee (Massachusetts State House); Paul Zaferiou (Washington Union Station); Lam Partners (Washington Metropolitan Area Transit Authority Stations); Pages 14–15 (left to right): Stephen Lee (David L. Lawrence Convention Center); Robert Benson Photography (Cleveland Clinic Cancer Institute); Bruce Damonte (SoFi Stadium); Page 98 (left to right): Warren Jagger (Beyond Walls); Kenny Clayton Photography (Cumberland Park); Richard S. Lee (Haddad Riverfront Park); Page 187: Ansel Olson (Main Street Station)

All rights reserved. Apart from any fair dealing for the purposes of private study, research, criticism or review as permitted under the Copyright Act, no part of this publication may be reproduced, stored in a retrieval system or transmitted in any form by any means, electronic, mechanical, photocopying, recording or otherwise, without the written permission of the publisher.

A catalogue record for this book is available from the National Library of Australia

Title: Lam Partners // The Many Ways of Light (Edited by Rebecca Gross)
ISBN: 9781864709292

This title was commissioned in IMAGES' Melbourne office and produced as follows: *Editorial* Georgia (Gina) Tsarouhas; Jeanette Wall; *Art direction and Production* Nicole Boehringer; *Layout* Margit Dittes Media, Germany

Printed on 150gsm GalerieArt Matt paper by DZS Grafik (Slovenia)

IMAGES has included on its website a page for special notices in relation to this and its other publications.
Please visit www.imagespublishing.com

Every effort has been made to trace the original source of copyright material contained in this book. The publishers would be pleased to hear from copyright holders to rectify any errors or omissions.
The information and illustrations in this publication have been prepared and supplied by Lam Partners in collaboration with Rebecca Gross. While all reasonable efforts have been made to ensure accuracy, the publishers do not, under any circumstances, accept responsibility for errors, omissions and representations express or implied.